**GOOD
GUYS
FINISH
FIRST**

GOOD GUYS FINISH FIRST

Success Strategies
from the Book of Proverbs
for Business Men and Women

Clinton W. McLemore

THE WESTMINSTER PRESS
Philadelphia

ACKNOWLEDGMENTS

Doubleday & Company, Inc., for verses from *The Jerusalem Bible,* copyright © 1966 by Darton, Longman & Todd Ltd. and Doubleday & Company, Inc.

National Council of the Churches of Christ in the U.S.A., for verses from the Revised Standard Version of the Bible copyrighted 1946, 1952, © 1971, 1973 by the Division of Christian Education of the National Council of the Churches of Christ in the U.S.A.

Oxford University Press and Cambridge University Press, for verses from *The New English Bible,* Copyright © The Delegates of the Oxford University Press and the Syndics of the Cambridge University Press 1961, 1970.

Tyndale House Publishers, for verses from *The Living Bible,* copyright 1971 by Tyndale House Publishers, Wheaton, Ill.

Zondervan Bible Publishers, for verses from the *Holy Bible: New International Version.* Copyright © 1978 by the New York International Bible Society.

First edition

BOOK DESIGN BY ALICE DERR

Bridgebooks
Published by The Westminster Press®
Philadelphia, Pennsylvania

PRINTED IN THE UNITED STATES OF AMERICA
9 8 7 6 5 4 3 2 1

Library of Congress Cataloging in Publication Data

McLemore, Clinton W., 1946–
  Good guys finish first.

  "Bridgebooks."
  Bibliography: p.
  1. Success. 2. Business ethics. I. Title.
HF5386.M475 1983   650.1   83–14708
ISBN 0–664–26004–7 (pbk.)

For
Gregory,
Karl,
and Kenneth

CONTENTS

ACKNOWLEDGMENTS

I would like to thank the following persons who, in one way or another, contributed to this book: Robert L. Toms, Senior Partner of Caldwell & Toms, for his wise and valuable counsel; my pastor, Lloyd John Ogilvie, for his support and encouragement of my work; Geddes MacGregor, Emeritus Distinguished Professor of Philosophy at the University of Southern California, who graciously read through the manuscript and made many helpful comments on it; Bryant B. Crouse, vice-president of Paul Stafford and Associates, for his ever-present intellectual inspiration and insistence that human decency would ultimately triumph over baseness; Jan Schafer, my secretary, for commenting constructively on the guidelines; and Laura Hobe, editor of Bridgebooks, for her expert editorial guidance.

C.W.M.

INTRODUCTION

This is a handbook for people in business. Whether you work for a large corporation, a small company, or directly for yourself, it is a manual to take with you into the trenches. It is for the executive as well as the entrepreneur, the secretary as well as the salesperson. No matter what one does, genuine success is built upon the same general principles.

GOOD GUYS FINISH FIRST is a survival guide as well as a prescription for success. Everything in this book rests on the assumption that survival and success are desirable, that there is *no* intrinsic merit to failing or falling, that thriving and achieving are *good.* Few people are ever called by God to be casualties.

Of course, if you have evil goals, attaining them will do no one any good, and if you are a terrible person, even your survival may not count for much. But I am not writing for terrible people or for those with sinister goals. This book is for people who want to better themselves and who are willing to put some serious effort into the process. My purpose is to provide you with high-quality information that you can actually use.

Unfortunately, the dominant trend these days in self-help books, including those written for business people, is to extol the wonders of selfishness. This trend seems to have been launched by Robert Ringer's *Winning Through Intimidation* (1974). In the introduction to his book, Ringer praises Ayn Rand's *Virtue of Selfishness* and quickly moves on to tell us how traditional virtues like honesty and hard work are myths that "do not work."

Ringer's themes were echoed in a series of books written by Michael Korda, the best known of which is *Power: How to Get It, How to Use It* (1975). Korda advises us on such technical matters as what kind of watch to wear (a thin, gold "power" one, of course) and whether to stand or sit at parties (never sit). Korda, however, is more temperate than Ringer. He even has a section on how nice guys finish first!

These kinds of books can be helpful, especially to certain people. The overly timid may well benefit from Ringer's exhortations to aggression.

And, there is surely profit in learning about status rituals and power games (you might as well know what you're up against).

The problem is that, even aside from issues of goodness and badness, such self-help guides DO NOT WORK. They tend to be simpleminded as well as shortsighted. As guiding principles for the business person, aggressiveness, gamesmanship, and narcissism just do not cut it! Even Gail Sheehy pointed out in her best-selling *Passages* that by the time most men are thirty they have discovered, the hard way, that the company values loyalty much more than it does dazzling displays of brilliance. I think most business people have always known deep, down inside that selfishness was self-defeating, but we are only beginning now to move beyond Ringer and Korda. Reality is once again setting in.

Civilization as we know it has been developing for a very long time. Throughout history, there have been persons who were specially gifted with wisdom. They knew what to do and why. Fortunately, their wisdom has been preserved for us in various documents. The existence of these documents makes it possible for us to learn directly from the wise of long ago. We can read how they thought and thus benefit from their insights. This, of course, is the great significance of books: the invention of writing and, later, of printing allowed information to be stored *outside* a human brain, in a permanent form. By reading books we can, as it were, inherit minds.

If one had to choose the book that most reflects the wisdom of our civilization, of its roots and heritage, it would have to be the Bible. Written over the course of roughly a thousand years, the Bible is actually a collection of more than sixty books. Its three quarters of a million words span a critical period in the formation of civilization: from when people were nomads trying to establish a stable society to when humanity began confronting, with sophistication, certain key existential questions. The Bible, therefore, gives us a series of historical portraits, including graphic descriptions of what gifted people came to understand about how to survive and succeed.

Of the many books contained within the Bible, Proverbs is most explicitly concerned with concrete advice. It tells us what to do. Many of the individual proverbs (wise sayings) are probably King Solomon's, who more than anyone in history is remembered for his sagacity. We even use the word "Solomonic" to refer to that which is very wise. Solomon, you may recall, was the ruler who divined which of two women was the true mother of an infant by ordering the child to be cut in two. The genuine mother, in an effort to avert tragedy, quickly asked Solomon to give her precious little one to the impostor.

Other proverbs represent the wisdom of persons whose names have long been lost. Who or exactly what they were no one knows for sure. What scholars have always agreed on, however, is that Proverbs is a most extraordinary book that seems as relevant today as it did thousands of years ago when it was put together. GOOD GUYS FINISH FIRST is an attempt to unpack fifty highly strategic proverbs—strategic because they have to do with strategies for survival and success.

Proverbs is a kind of textbook, intended largely to instruct up-and-comers. It tells how to prosper, how to stay out of trouble, how to handle difficult people. On the other hand, Proverbs is not put together the way contemporary Western texts are: carefully organized, each point following from the last, lots of illustrations, and so on. To the twentieth-century reader, it sometimes appears to be a disorganized collection of unrelated truisms, a mere hodgepodge. This, however, it is not. Neither is it an atlas of cheap and clever tricks for taking advantage of others.

However jumbled up Proverbs may seem to the casual reader, it points relentlessly to the FUNDAMENTAL TENDENCY FOR GOODNESS AND PROSPERITY TO GO TOGETHER. *This* is the universal principle glaringly missing in many of the self-help manuals. Bad people do occasionally prosper—as books like *The Godfather* suggest—and good people do occasionally "lose." Nevertheless, it remains as true today as it did in King Solomon's time that graciousness and integrity, coupled with the right measure of prudence, actually HELP one to do well. "Good guys finish last" is sometimes just an excuse for personal failure or, worse, a flimsy justification for ruthlessness.

I hope that you will find this book a reliable ally as you make your way through what can be, at times, the jungle of modern business. It is designed to be a true friend, a source of inspiration, and a trustworthy companion, there to assist at a moment's notice.

The pages to follow will, I hope, assist you in viewing today's world—indeed, your work world—through the rich lenses of wisdom to be found in Scripture.

A READER'S GUIDE

Contrary to instant this and instant that, few worthwhile things come without effort. To get the most out of this book, carry it with you, in your briefcase, pocketbook, lunch pail, or wherever. When you get a few spare moments, take GOOD GUYS out and read a little of it.

Familiarity is the key to profiting from this material. You have to go over it again and again, until it becomes a part of you. It is not enough to read a few lines today and a few more a month from now. While anything is obviously better than nothing, you will draw far more from these lessons —which is what they are—if you immerse yourself in them. How does one best do this? Drawing on some general principles from the psychology of learning, I would like to offer these suggestions:

First, go through the whole book quickly to get an overview of what it contains. You might skim it in a half hour or, if you prefer, read the book through in one or two sittings. This kind of initial *survey* will give you "hooks" upon which to hang related ideas. Time spent in this way will yield high dividends later. But don't stop there.

Among the best aids to internalizing new information is *repetition,* which is the second principle to follow. Take a portion of the book and read it through. Then, in a few days or a week, read it through again. You will soon get to the point where you will have to read only the individual proverbs, since you will remember what I have written for each one. By the same token, probably none of us will ever so internalize the proverbs themselves as no longer to need to read them now and then. GOOD GUYS should, therefore, be a book you can use for many years.

The third principle to keep in mind is that what psychologists call "spaced practice" is usually better than "massed practice." It is often better to study one hour today and one hour tomorrow, for example, than two hours in a row today. Naturally there are exceptions, times when doing it all at once works best. Find out what suits your individual rhythm of learning. In general, most people do best with *distributed practice.*

Next, *read actively.* As often as possible, I have tried to encourage this by posing questions about how the guidelines might apply to your life. Take this even further if you can. Research has amply demonstrated that the more emotionally meaningful the material, the better it will be remembered. The easiest way to make anything emotionally meaningful is to relate it to your own life. Question everything. "Is that true?" "Do I buy that?" "When have I observed this sort of thing happening in my life?" "In other people's lives?" "Are there times when the opposite seems to be true?" Write comments in the book as a way to interact with it. Rate yourself on each guideline in the space provided.

All of this takes more energy than casual reading, but the effort you invest will yield favorable results. Question, reflect, apply. The more, the better.

Finally, keep a record of how many times you study each guideline. You can do this in a number of ways, the simplest of which is to put a check next to a guideline each time you work with it. Such elementary record-keeping will give you a definite sense of accomplishment and suggest where you may need to put most of your efforts in the future.

Scripture is alive! Like Jacob with the angel (Genesis 32), wrestle with it until it blesses YOU.

FUNDAMENTAL GRACIOUSNESS

GUIDELINE 1

The tongue has power of life and death; make friends with it and enjoy its fruits (Proverbs 18:21, NEB).

"Your brother Harry, of course, has always been smarter than you."

"Well, it's just your personality. You know. You're just not . . ."

"Look, buddy. I don't care whether you're the boss or not. I think you're a total jerk!"

In this age of assertiveness training and looking out for number one, the value of simple graciousness is often underestimated. As nearly all etiquette books point out, basic decency underlies many of our proper customs. At the root of good manners is a good heart—concern for the other person.

The most important aspect of manners, good or bad, is what we say. Accordingly, Guideline 1 highlights the awesome power of the tongue. As this ancient saying indicates, people have died because of what they or others said or failed to say. Words are incredibly potent. They can build and give life. They can tear down and destroy. Unfortunately, it is almost always easier to destroy than to create.

Proverbs contains a whole series of sayings about loose or otherwise improper talk. We will examine them in some detail in Section 4. Here, let us just note the emphasis that the writer of this particular proverb places on "making friends" with our tongue. It is as if the tongue were an unruly relative with which we were forced to live. There is no choice but to tame it. Once tamed, the tongue becomes a wonderful tool. Correctly used, the tongue will yield bountiful fruit on our behalf.

Misled by amateur stick-up-for-yourself psychology, many people believe that the best way to ensure success is to bully others. "Speak up. Don't let yourself be walked on. Let 'em have it! Demand exactly what you want."

Such strategies may have their place, and they will certainly get you what you want in many situations. But they can be lethal to long-term relationships, whether at home or in the office. Many promising executives have been permanently promoted "down the hall" where no one ever saw them again, simply because they were rude or careless in what they said to whom. These once rising "stars" did not understand the tremendous power of words. I once watched a door-to-door salesman use his tongue to intimidate potential buyers. They almost always bought something the first time he came to their door, but from then on out he could never find his "customers" home. They were chronically "out." Such can be the result of callous assertion!

Most successful people, especially those with major executive responsibilities, are far more smooth than abrasive. They artfully craft what they say, well knowing how important this is to their effectiveness. They realize, in the words of another proverb (16:24, NEB), "Kind words are like dripping honey."

This proverb is not advocating verbal treachery or devious manipulation. As we shall see, a central theme of Proverbs is the wisdom of avoiding all forms of treachery and deceit, which eventually seem to come back to haunt us. This guideline is intended to put us in mind of the power of communication. Words, though invisible, can be starkly real in their effects.

Persons who justify verbal insensitivity in the name of candor usually fool only themselves. What some persons try to dignify or excuse with the term "honesty," others recognize as boorishness. Verbal brutality is socially ineffective if not self-destructive. Cut others with the lash of your tongue and, when they can, they will often try to hurt you back. Build them up with sincere words and they will reward you. The next time you are tempted to "let someone have it," count the potential costs. There *are* times to assert yourself but, in general, confrontation is a risky strategy.

Is there someone at this moment you are tempted to tell off?
Is there a better way to accomplish your goal?
Is there someone you ought to build up with your words?

SELF-EVALUATION RATING: 1   2   3   4   5
  (circle one number, 5 = best)

NOTES AND REFLECTIONS:

GUIDELINE 2

He who conceals another's offence seeks his goodwill, but he who harps on something breaks up friendship (Proverbs 17:9, NEB).

Most of us have a strong tendency to relish the sensational. For complex psychological reasons, we like the shocking, the scandalous, even the sordid. Within the business world, where competition prevails, our lust for the sensational can prove overpowering, since the other person's blunders and mishaps make us look all the better by comparison.

"Did you hear what Johnson did?"

"Remember the Miller account? Well, Barton just lost it!"

"That's not my fault. Harrison's the one who didn't get the stuff in on time."

A very successful friend of mine has developed such a reputation for business savvy that many young executives go to him when they need advice. Often they will ask him general questions about how to "make it" in what they perceive—with some justification—as shark-infested waters. Because my friend is such a seasoned warrior of corporate combat who, in his words, has gotten "a lot of blood on his own shirt," his advice tends to astonish them: "Make the other guy the hero."

Such advice is the exact opposite of much contemporary how-to-succeed-in-business counsel. Typically we are advised to engineer our own grandeur. "If there's any chance they're going to hand out swords to fall on, make sure that the person next to you is seen as a more worthy recipient." We are even advised to spread whatever gossip may prove necessary to ensure that his or her "worthiness" is noticed!

The relationship in which loyalty is most important is the one with your own boss. MAKE THE BOSS LOOK GOOD. Don't detract from his or her prestige by claiming credit for everything you do. SERVE.

Recall the fable about the lion and the mouse. According to the fable, a mouse finds herself caught under one of the huge paws of the ferocious beast. "Please," begs the mouse, "let me go and someday I may be able to repay you." Reluctantly, and only after scoffing at the obvious absurdity of such a little creature ever being able to help such a majestic beast, the lion complies. Some time later, the lion becomes hopelessly ensnared in a hunter's net. The mouse appears and, by chewing through the ropes, repays in kind the lion's earlier benevolence.

When someone around us is vulnerable, we temporarily become the lion. In the fast-moving world of business, however, lions quickly become mice and vice versa.

In advising us to conceal others' offenses, the author of this proverb is not advocating perjury or martyrdom. He *is* recommending kindness: don't opportunistically make a big deal out of someone else's blunder. Facilitate the *other* person's glory. Work for the other person's good. By advertising others' blunders, you tend to lose friends and allies. In business, such losses are potentially fatal. Lose enough allies and you may lose your job. Even if you own the company, you may lose valuable employees or accounts.

Few people in business know the enormous potential of casting what others do in the *best* possible light.

Whose "offences" might you cover?
Whom could you help to become a hero?

SELF-EVALUATION RATING: 1   2   3   4   5

NOTES AND REFLECTIONS:

GUIDELINE 3

It is to a man's honour if he avoids quarrels, but fools never exercise self-control (Proverbs 20:3, JB).

Imagine that you are asked to gather some information, perhaps related to an important job your company has to do. You conscientiously collect it, meticulously arrange it for presentation, and deliver the finished product. There is no question in your mind that you have done your duty with distinction and that absolutely no one could have done it any better.

Now suppose that after all this someone viciously attacks your report. Your critic calls it "incomplete," which most certainly it is not, as well as "sloppy" and "superficial." Beyond this, after spending many extra hours on the project, for which you will not receive a penny, you are even called "lazy." What would your reaction be?

Many people would, at this point, blow. It would not matter if the critic were the president, a co-worker, or the firm's best customer, their reactions would be violent. Instead of remaining cool, they would feel it necessary to defend their honor.

An acquaintance of mine has an index card posted on his bedroom mirror. On it are typed the words, "YOU ARE NOT THE TARGET," taken from a book by that title. This is a difficult concept to bear in mind when someone is maligning you or your work. It is hard not to take such insults personally. However, NOT personalizing irrational attacks is, in fact, what effective leaders are able to do. Contrary to widespread opinion, most successful business people are not often combative. They know better!

Regardless of how things may seem at the moment, your worst antagonists may not be out to get YOU. People sometimes attack the person nearest to them, or simply the person who seems least likely or able to retaliate. However unfair, this happens a great deal in business. The issue is whether such unfairness can hook you into a senseless battle.

The late psychiatrist Karen Horney (died 1952) pointed to the dangers of what she called "neurotic pride." (Something is neurotic when it does not work, e.g., it does not get us the security and self-esteem we desire, but we do it over and over again anyway.) She noted that almost all of us maintain an idealized conception of ourselves which, if challenged, leads to a sense of outrage, a feeling of "how dare they!" Some people, for example, fly into a rage if anyone questions their integrity. Others start swinging if their "manhood" is threatened. The more neurotic pride we harbor, the more inflexible our behavior becomes.

A major difference between humans and animals is that our behavior is ordinarily more versatile, more adaptive, more responsive to the situations in which we find ourselves. Interestingly, *The New English Bible* translates the second half of Guideline 3 as, "it is the fool who bares his teeth."

People in many parts of the world telegraph their aggressive intentions by exposing and sometimes clenching their teeth. This is exactly what large primates do, which is why it is not always a good idea to smile at gorillas (especially if they are close enough to grab hold of you!). The author of this proverb is telling us to act flexibly as a human being, not reflexively as an ape.

The trouble with reflexive aggression is that, with it, you can add fuel to an already explosive mixture. Interpersonal combustion can occur rapidly and, before you know it, you are caught up in a terrible blaze. Most murders occur not on the streets but in the kitchen. Few people who have committed such a murder ever saw it coming. Like the protagonist in Camus's *The Stranger,* we can easily become the victims of bizarre circumstance, with the result that our lives can be radically and permanently changed.

Whenever you possibly can, back away from hostile disputes, so that you do not become the unwitting target of someone else's neurosis. Maintain your poise. Retain your flexibility. No macho stuff. No getting hooked.

What sorts of criticisms or challenges most easily get you into senseless arguments?
What could you do to avoid such arguments the next time someone pushes the buttons of *your* neurotic pride?

SELF-EVALUATION RATING: 1   2   3   4   5

NOTES AND REFLECTIONS:

GUIDELINE 4

To answer a question before you have heard it out is both stupid and insulting (Proverbs 18:13, NEB).

*"Let's get on with it." This is usually what is in my mind when I answer someone's question before I have fully heard it. Occasionally I finish the question, answer it, and then discover that I have answered the wrong question.

Unlike people from some other cultures, we are extremely time conscious. We treat time as a precious commodity whose value is lost unless we efficiently spend it. Because the central business value of productivity is defined as "output per unit time," work tends to be one endless game of beat the clock.

Unfortunately, the game can be lethal. Medical psychologists suggest that certain personality characteristics tend to be associated with coronary disease. These Type A traits include competitiveness and the tendency to rush. Hence, the "stupidity" to which the proverb writer refers may be more than social. Finishing other people's questions may be a sign that we are also finishing off ourselves. The author of this proverb is, I believe, commenting on a general frame of mind. We are being warned against hyperactivity.

Cutting others off is fundamentally disrespectful. It tells them that we care more about the information they have, or even about the information that we think we have, than we do about them. Although people rarely say it, they almost always feel punished when they are cut off. Thus, underneath the momentum of any conversation in which one person is pushing the other, there is going to be some resentment. We all want to be listened to, to feel that what we have to say is important.

People vary in their temperaments, however, and therefore some of us are more impatient than others. There may be strong biological contributions to these temperament differences. Even newborn babies show wide variations in their activity levels. Some are slow and easy, others are jumpy and tense. Adults, of course, show similar differences.

If you are one of the fast people, you will probably have trouble letting slow people communicate at their own rate. Always you will want to hurry them along. Yet it is important to realize that some people who speak slowly think remarkably quickly! Speech rate is not always indicative of intelligence. So, even aside from the disrespect of adding your words to someone else's question, pushing may cause you to miss some very important information.

Graciousness is sometimes a great aid to intelligence. By listening patiently, you can usually penetrate more deeply into issues. Careful reflection almost always triumphs, sooner or later, over flashy wit and quick conversation. Moreover, by surrendering to time pressure—the pressure to get on with it—you can easily spiral yourself down into a pit of anxiety. Sometimes the more you rush, the more you feel the need to rush. You let your psychological center of gravity get outside of yourself and then spend the rest of the day trying to recapture it.

Professional interviewers have discovered something that runs counter to our natural expectations: communication usually becomes more effective as it becomes *less* focused. In other words, more information will be exchanged if people can communicate the way they want to. Naturally, if you want a specific answer, you need a specific question, such as "When will you turn in your next budget?" Most of the time, however, communication goes *up* as freedom of expression goes up for *both* parties.

As an experiment, make an effort to let others finish their own questions. Try making yourself wait three seconds after they finish their questions before you begin talking. It may be hard to do, but I think you will like the resulting peace of mind—which is probably NOT what you feel when you rush others.

Whose questions do you most often finish?
How much do each of these people like you?
Are you satisfied with your own style?

SELF-EVALUATION RATING: 1   2   3   4   5

NOTES AND REFLECTIONS:

GUIDELINE 5

A gift opens the way for the giver and ushers him into the presence of the great (Proverbs 18:16, NIV); A gift given in secret soothes anger (Proverbs 21:14a, NIV).

Suppose you wanted to meet the president of a large corporation. How would you go about it?

If you were fortunate enough to know someone who knew the president, you might simply ask your acquaintance to give you an introduction. But suppose you were not so fortunate. You could try sending a gift. Gifts have tremendous symbolic value. They tend to be loaded with meaning for us, perhaps because we long to return to childhood when we were given presents as expressions of adult love. The best gifts are probably those that have the most symbolic value to the persons receiving them. Such value is not always reflected in a high price tag.

Perhaps, for instance, you knew that the corporation president was raised in India and collected miniature elephants. A few hours rummaging through resale shops could turn up something inexpensive that he or she might nonetheless treasure.

Even a note of appreciation might, in some circumstances, prove a suitable "gift." I have found over and over again that writing sincere notes of appreciation to eminent people almost always makes them receptive to a personal visit.

The proverb writer is NOT recommending insincerity. As we shall see, many proverbs overtly attack flattery and other forms of deceit. He is simply advising us to express our goodwill tangibly.

Let us consider another situation. Suppose someone was very angry with you and you wanted to assuage this anger. You could, of course, simply apologize. Apologies do not always work, however, partly because "words are cheap" and partly because verbal communications to rageful people sometimes only augment their fury. Again, you could quietly send a gift. You might, for example, have something sent that you know the person would like—a radio, a book, a basket of goodies, flowers, whatever. The note attached might well say from you and nothing else. The other person might remain angry, but at very least you would probably constructively throw him or her off balance for a moment.

People who are angry usually feel, at root, frustrated and helpless. We tend to get angry with anything that threatens to hurt us. When people are angry with us, they typically feel that we have somehow cheated them. Giving gifts to these people can restore their sense of being treated fairly, which of course can tame them and increase their happiness. Friends do this sort of thing all the time. Whenever one of two good friends has been neglectful, for example, he or she will more readily agree to something the other wants.

The catch is that you have to give the gift without fanfare. Otherwise the angry person is likely to feel awkward or embarrassed and, as a result, turn on you! Your good intentions will be rewarded only with pain. You have to make sure that the gift is more or less casual, that it does not cause any loss of face, any feeling of being patronized or babied.

Remember that gifts are symbols of appreciation and esteem. Symbols are carriers of implicit meaning. If you make symbols too explicit, they lose their value. Hence, "I am giving you this nice gift to cool you off" is not likely to prove effective.

It is usually difficult to give to someone who is angry with us. That person's anger tends to put us on the defensive, even to kindle our anger. This is precisely the time to give, to soften, to do the unexpected.

Some small investments yield big dividends. The giving of gifts can be like that.

To whom in your life might you wisely give a tastefully chosen gift? Whose anger might you soothe with a present?

SELF-EVALUATION RATING: 1   2   3   4   5

NOTES AND REFLECTIONS:

GUIDELINE 6

Refuse no man any favour that you owe him when it lies in your power to pay it (Proverbs 3:27, NEB).

It is sometimes very hard to bring ourselves to pay certain kinds of debts. Most people pay their bills on time, partly because they know that their credit ratings will be impaired if they do not. But it is sometimes harder to work up the motivation to repay favors. Knowing that this time it will be our turn to pay the check, do we not upon occasion go to lunch with certain people only reluctantly?

Almost all human transactions, especially in business, rest on trust. Every time you write someone a check or hand someone a charge card, you are asking that person to trust you. Every time someone accepts such promissory items, he or she is agreeing to grant you this trust. Even the gas or electric company supplies energy to your residence ONLY because its directors believe that you will pay for what you use. Democracy itself is ultimately based on such trust.

To refuse to pay a debt is shortsighted opportunism. You win in the short run, but everybody may lose in the end. Society cannot run on breached contracts. Most everyday contracts involve the exchange of promises. To break a promise is usually to forfeit your honor. Even if no one brings the matter to your attention, your trustworthiness will from that point forward be at issue.

Sometimes our responsibilities for payment become very subtle. For example, if people work for you, there is always at least an implicit understanding that you will reward those who carry out their duties with distinction. There may be no written or oral contract. You may never have announced any kind of special bonus for those who do well. Nevertheless, it is simply an unspoken assumption in business that the boss will reward the worthy. As another translation of this proverb states, "Do not withhold good from those to whom it is due, when it is in your power to do it" (RSV).

There are, of course, many kinds of rewards. Money is the most obvious reward, but there is also promotion, appreciation, and recognition. The good manager is one who knows which reward to give, and when. Judd Swihart, a friend of mine, wrote a book in which he suggests that there are at least eight "languages of love." There is the giving of presents, the verbal expression of affection, the physical demonstration of love, and so forth. Good lovers tailor their choice of language to the needs and desires of the other person. Sometimes a simple word of praise is far more effective than the most lavish trinket.

"Jan, thank you. Thanks for staying late and typing all that stuff."

"Jeri, I appreciate the time off you gave me last week. Is there something I can do for you?"

"Dave, there's only one thing wrong with this article we're publishing together. You deserve to be the first author."

To withhold what you owe another is to steal. It is also to slight. People will not maintain their loyalties to you if you steal from and slight them. They will feel ripped off and resentful. All of this can go on without ever being mentioned. Nevertheless, how you ACT in the face of debt to them will speak loudly indeed.

Try to ensure that others see you as trustworthy and honorable, as worthy of their loyalty and affection. Since few of us fulfill all of our social responsibilities, making a deliberate effort to do so will surely enhance your standing as a person and as a leader. People will like you, respect you, and regard you as a true friend.

To whom, if anyone, do you owe something?
To whom can you grant a "good" that is deserved?

SELF-EVALUATION RATING: 1   2   3   4   5

NOTES AND REFLECTIONS:

GUIDELINE 7

Open rebuke is better than hidden love! (Proverbs 27:5, TLB).

A psychologist I know once worked for another psychologist who, unfortunately, could not bring himself to affirm his subordinates. The senior psychologist is a good man whom I personally like but who, like most of us, is less than perfect. He does not know how to give "strokes."

Neither does he seem fully to grasp how much productivity his "hidden love" is losing him and the organization for which he works. Many of his people spend time wondering, worrying, and complaining which they could better spend working. A brief compliment to each of them now and then would probably improve his managerial effectiveness by 100 percent.

Some managers deliberately keep their subordinates off balance, on the theory that "keeping people anxious" improves their performance. Usually it does not. Industrial research seems clearly to indicate that frightening people increases productivity only when they are doing such monotonous tasks as piecework and when the manager can monitor their output. For the jobs that most people do, whether it involves creating spreadsheets or filing folders, insecurity drives them quickly to distraction.

I have even heard a psychologist defend his own deprivational style by arguing that giving people only a little reinforcement is probably best. He was reasoning, I assume, on the basis of what is known as "the partial reinforcement effect." This is the principle that "organisms" will continue to do something longer *after* the goodies stop if these goodies were previously given inconsistently. A rat that has been fed for pressing a bar only once in a while, for example, will continue to press it for a longer time when the food totally stops than a rat that has been rewarded every time for bar-pressing. People, however, are not rats. Even if they were, bar-pressing is definitely more like factory piecework than perusing budgets or D & B reports.

Managers who believe in emotionally starving their subordinates should read *The Prince*. This early sixteenth-century classic, written by Nicolò Machiavelli, warns against ruling by threat. Such management works, if it ever does, only as long as you retain your power. Lose it for even a little while and, since you have built up no affection for yourself in the hearts of the managed, they may tear you to bits.

Even assuming that the people around you do not fear you, they cannot live on your unexpressed appreciation. Everyone needs affirmation. Without it they wither and start to act in strange and unproductive ways. Their attention turns away from their jobs, toward finding ways to meet their needs for validation.

To respond with "I value you even though I don't say so" is to present a very weak case. You may possess warehouses of wonderful food, all purchased with me in mind, but if you do not feed me some of it, I could die! Generals engender the loyalty of their troops by making sure they get their provisions.

Some people *know* that it is good to affirm others, but they just cannot bring themselves to do it. If you have difficulty expressing positive feelings, admit it to yourself and then do something about it. Start practicing. Begin with something easy, such as, "That's a pretty coat you're wearing," or even something easier like a simple "Thank you." See if you can work up to, "You know, I think you're a terrific human being!"

Toward whom, if anyone, have you not expressed the appreciation you genuinely feel?

SELF-EVALUATION RATING: 1   2   3   4   5

NOTES AND REFLECTIONS:

SOME NECESSARY CAUTION

GUIDELINE 8

Good intelligence wins favour, but treachery leads to disaster (Proverbs 13:15, NEB); The wise man sees evil coming and avoids it (Proverbs 14:16, JB).

"Don't cross the line," the writer of the first proverb seems to be saying. "Don't get too smart for your own good."

In my psychotherapy practice, I have occasionally worked with truly brilliant people who used their brainpower for perverse ends. One boy with whom I worked was, by anyone's standards, extraordinarily intelligent. Unfortunately, for a number of his adolescent years, he used his cortical endowment to mastermind thefts. Again and again he paid a stiff price for this misapplication of his giftedness.

Intelligence is a tool, sometimes a weapon. Using your intelligence without any direction is like shooting at random. Using your intelligence for treachery is more like assassination. Assassins are often despised by the very people who hire them, and many are themselves assassinated! Predators often end up as prey.

What exactly is intelligence? Although technical definitions vary, most include the idea that intelligence involves the capacity to learn and to reason. Another way to put this is that intelligence is the ability to acquire information and to solve problems. Intelligence is the talent for acquiring and organizing knowledge.

Wisdom, on the other hand, has to do with the judicious application of knowledge to everyday affairs. A person may be able to do higher mathematics faster than anyone else on earth and still not be wise. Such a person may continually allow himself or herself to be swindled or to jump from one bad relationship to another. Yet, some relatively dull people are remarkably wise. They know how to live. What they know about arithmetic might not impress anyone, but they have insight—they are able to see—into practical matters and to make good decisions about them.

As the author of the second proverb suggests, a central attribute of the wise person is the avoidance of evil. Naturally you cannot avoid what you do not see, so wisdom in this sense clearly involves what we described above as intelligence. Nonetheless, to see evil coming and still walk into its clutches has to be the quintessence of foolishness.

But what is evil and exactly what is so dangerous about getting involved in it? Just as there has been debate over the best definition of intelligence, great scholars have argued over how evil should be defined. Is evil a thing in itself, or is it merely the absence of good?

Again, we will not try to resolve such issues here. For our purposes, let us just posit that to do something evil is to do something that has the potential to damage someone seriously. The reason that the proverb writer tells us, in effect, that it is wise to avoid evil is that, if we do not, there is a very good chance that we will be among its victims.

I know someone who, in order to increase the yearly sales volume of his business, linked himself up with some unsavory characters. He found himself in more and more difficult predicaments, until eventually he lost control of a business that he had worked very hard to build.

Evil is like heated tar. Touch it and suddenly it is all over you, attached to everything you do, everything you own, everything you stand for, even everything you think and feel.

Use your intelligence for good and keep away from anything unsavory, whether treachery or some other self-toxic activity. If you are currently stuck in the tar, choose a good adviser and begin the process of extricating yourself from it.

With what particular kinds of intelligence are you most blessed?
How can you make the best use of these gifts?
What specific evils do you need to make sure you avoid?

SELF-EVALUATION RATING: 1   2   3   4   5

NOTES AND REFLECTIONS:

GUIDELINE 9

Impatience runs into folly; distinction comes by careful thought (Proverbs 14:17, NEB).

Suppose you are in a meeting and an important issue is under discussion. At some point you want to influence the decision that has to be made. What should you say and when should you say it?

Ironically, the more you care about an issue, the more likely you are to speak prematurely. More times than I can count, I have rushed in when I should have waited. Clearly, if you wait too long to board the train, you will be standing on the platform as it pulls away. If you board without forethought, however, you might end up on the wrong train. A great deal is in the timing.

A colleague of mine has a habit of waiting until all the others say what they have to say before he speaks. He will then gesture to the chairperson, perhaps by raising only his index finger. He is almost always immediately recognized. Sometimes I think that if he were sitting in a fine New York restaurant far away from the kitchen and suddenly whispered for the chef, out would come someone in a white hat. Once my colleague is recognized, he waits about three seconds—they seem like hours!—before he begins to speak. By this time the room of about fifteen people is silent, hanging, waiting to hear the first word. Partly because of this well-practiced social style, he is a very effective communicator.

Impulsiveness often leaves you looking, if not acting, silly. Trial attorneys understand this very well. They will deliberately needle witnesses for the other side in order to get them upset. Once this happens, the credibility of the witness is reduced appreciably. The implication is: "If this witness can't even keep cool under cross-examination, how could you possibly rely on anything he or she says? Why, this person is unstable." Such a conclusion may not be fair, but it is often drawn by jurors.

"Careful thought" requires patience, the opposite of impulsiveness. Patience is, among other things, the ability to endure tension, to live with unpleasantness or uncertainty instead of rushing in to do something. When we say or do things in business primarily to reduce our inner discomforts, it will almost always backfire.

Most accidents occur because someone fails to think before acting. Someone pulls out of a driveway without looking. Someone changes lanes on the highway before making sure that it is safe to do so. Someone decides to take that chance which ultimately turns out to be fatal. It is no different in business. Although once in a while an impulsive move will later show itself to have been sheer genius, such moves have ruined far more careers than they have enhanced.

Impatience is like a disease that, if untreated, gets worse. This is because doing something (almost anything) when you feel tense usually reduces your level of tension. Lowering tension, of course, is pleasant ("reinforcing"). Because doing something leads to the relief of tension, you are all the more likely to do something the next time. To end this self-perpetuating cycle, it is important to STOP yourself from such escapism. Instead of scrambling to end your tensions, stay with them for a while. Get to know them.

By attending carefully to your own inner psychological processes, you can begin to train yourself in the art of patience. You can, as it were, sneak up on yourself, on your proclivity to leap before looking. In the process you will actually be practicing "careful thought."

Remember: from careful thought comes distinction.

How much "distinction" do you currently enjoy because you are known for your careful thought?

What sorts of issues are most likely to prompt you to become impatient and, thus, push you into the realm of folly?

SELF-EVALUATION RATING: 1   2   3   4   5

NOTES AND REFLECTIONS:

GUIDELINE 10

Be timid in business and come to beggary; be bold and make a fortune (Proverbs 11:16b, NEB).

Patience and timidity are not the same thing. To be patient is to weigh alternatives until you know what you should say or do. To be timid is to be unable to act even after you know. "Go for it," the proverb writer is urging. "Once you know what to do, move ahead without vacillation."

What would you do if you had a business idea, say, a new invention, which you were convinced could be extremely successful? Out of fear would you procrastinate? Or would you take the risk of failing, which is actually the only road to success?

A friend of mine, when he was in his late thirties, decided that he was finally going to do what he had always wanted to do: launch out on his own. Having worked as an engineer for many years designing automotive products, he had the training and experience to do this sort of creative work with true expertise. With his wife's support, he mortgaged everything and moved forward. What he did, in fact, was to place himself in a position where he *had* to succeed. There was no room left for timidity!

What happened is one of those success-in-American-business stories. There is a reasonably good chance that *your* car is equipped with one of his accessories.

If his story makes you envious—sometimes it makes me envious!—keep in mind that everyone has a different calling. You might not enjoy spending your life making and marketing automotive parts. But there is no doubt something you would enjoy, and the question is whether you are doing it.

Let me emphasize that family men should not ordinarily drop everything they are doing, and risk everything they have, to pursue imaginary money trees. Such behavior is not much different from risking your entire net worth at the racetrack. You might win briefly but, in the long run, you will very likely go home with your pockets empty. It is worth noting that many compulsive gamblers, people who eventually wind up borrowing or even stealing money which they inevitably lose, won big the first time out. Like compulsive gamblers, some business people do not know when to quit. If the deck is stacked against you, the time to quit, of course, is before you begin. Many business persons have been ruined by their infatuations with harebrained schemes.

Investment analysts are forever pointing out that good investors know when to sell. Part of the lore of Wall Street, for example, is that "good traders take their losses." If they have purchased a bad security, they get rid of it, even if they are behind. Most investors do not do this because they do not like losing. They tend to hang on to their bad stocks and sell off their good ones. So, you have to be flexible and, as another friend of mine says, stay unattached. If the venture is clearly bad, get out of it or, even better, never get into it.

The other side of this analysis, however, reads like this: good investors are courageous. Not foolish, just venturesome. They willingly take risks when the conditions are promising. Sometimes they win and sometimes they lose, but they do not have to lecture themselves in the mirror for lacking initiative. Others tend to see them as having both brains and guts.

I should add that all proverbs are generalizations. Hence, you cannot assume that boldness alone will guarantee prosperity. We need to balance the gambler's daring with the sage's circumspection. The goal is to have both prowess and prudence. As a legendary frontiersman put it, "Be sure you're right, then go ahead." By all means, do go ahead!

At this point in your career, how do you assess your level of risk-taking? Is there something you would like to accomplish that seems to be hindered only by your timidity?

SELF-EVALUATION RATING: 1   2   3   4   5

NOTES AND REFLECTIONS:

A king's threat is like a lion's roar; one who ignores it is his own worst enemy (Proverbs 20:2, NEB).

Some people are so out of it that they truly do not comprehend even the most obvious dangers. Somehow they just miss the fact that certain things, or certain people, can hurt them. But this proverb is really about something else: authority problems.

Because I worked for years as a psychological consultant for a vocational guidance center, I have done a great deal of psychological assessment on persons with career troubles. Many of the people I have evaluated were in mid-career and distressed over not having achieved what they had hoped. Sometimes they had been fired, sometimes just not promoted. Whatever the reason, they were attempting with our help to take a careful look at their own lives. In many cases, they were edging toward, if not rushing into, a job change.

The information I obtained through my assessment often indicated that the client had trouble getting along with those in authority. Sometimes the client knew this, but typically he or she did not. Often the person would rationalize (make excuses for) his or her inability to relate to superiors.

"Oh, that guy was a real idiot. No one could do anything right according to him."

"But," I would ask, "what about the other three bosses you have had?"

"They weren't much better. Let me tell you about . . ."

Just about anyone will follow someone whose authority he or she perceives as legitimate. People with authority problems, however, do not readily grant such legitimacy. They do not automatically give respect, and thus obedience, to others simply because of the positions, and hence the power, they hold. Such people demand that authorities prove themselves worthy.

Every one of us has, at one time or another, been "judged and found wanting by our inferiors." The best and most able people do not always end up with the most power. Almost daily we are faced with the challenge of getting along with people who, despite the fact that they have power over us, may be far less qualified than we are. The king, in other words, may be incompetent.

This proverb is exhorting us to open our eyes and reckon with what is before us. "Look," the writer seems to be saying, "the king [or the boss] can hurt you. Don't ignore his [her] threats by sticking your head in the sand and pretending that he [she] cannot. If you do not acknowledge the realities of power, you are your own worst enemy."

People who "ignore the king's threat" are often motivated by their own destructive psychodynamics. Something going on inside of them is so driving that it impairs their ability to deal with reality. They are ever ready to do battle with "the big guy," the guy who carries the badge or signs the time cards. "No one is going to talk to them like that."

When you scratch the surface of authority problems, you often discover that the person is really trying to work out a problem with someone from the past, usually a parent. The police person or the plant manager is just an unconscious substitute. The person is actually angry with Mom or Dad.

Probe one level deeper and you usually discover that, underneath the anger, there is fear. The individual is *afraid* of the king! Underneath all that rebellion are painful memories and a related fear of further punishment, psychological or physical.

If you find yourself in conflict with those in power, especially if this is a recurrent theme in your life, see if you can determine what (or whom) you may *fear*. Are you really fighting your father, your mother, your uncle, your aunt, your sister, your brother? Don't dismiss these questions without addressing them honestly, because a lot of this may be subconscious for you. Try to remember that fear underlies almost all anger.

To what extent do you ignore "the king's threat"?
Would you have the courage to admit that you were afraid if you were?

SELF-EVALUATION RATING: 1   2   3   4   5

NOTES AND REFLECTIONS:

GUIDELINE 12

Never be one to give guarantees, or to pledge yourself as surety for another (Proverbs 22:26, NEB).

The author of the proverb is saying, in essence, "Hold on to your power." Your money and your freedom are both forms of power. Do not relinquish them casually. Do not obligate yourself in self-destructive ways. Don't put everything on the line for someone else, unless there is a very good reason to do so.

There is another message in this proverb. As hard as it may be, and as hardhearted as it may sound, sometimes you just have to let others take the consequences of their own actions. You cannot always bail them out of trouble. If you try to, not only will you probably end up in trouble yourself but *they* never learn to take care of themselves. Overprotectiveness only fosters unhealthy dependence and pathetic immaturity.

Like just about every other clinical psychologist in the country, I have worked with many parents who had great difficulty ending their own over-protective behavior. One particular couple had raised an adopted son whose foremost expression of gratitude was repeatedly to get into trouble. Time after time they rescued him. Although they were not always conversant with the latest fad in child rearing (thank God), they really loved that kid! Finally, they stopped rescuing him. Within six months he straightened himself out. Sometimes if you want to help someone, you have to refuse to help.

Such advice can, of course, be used as an excuse for never helping anyone. This, obviously, is not the purpose of the proverb. Its author is simply trying to educate us about the *lack* of wisdom in always rushing in to fix things.

Perhaps because I have been trained to be a helper, I have often—much too often—tried to fix things for people. As therapist, I have often seen what a person ought to do for his or her own good. Always I have wanted these people to see it too . . . and to do it!

People, however, need time to grow. They need to work out their own lives. There are reasons, sometimes deep and complicated ones, for why people come to be in the situations they do. Efforts to save them can be frustrating and naive.

I once worked with a very gifted young psychologist who, time and again, got himself into trouble with the power structure under which we both worked. This did not hurt his career very much in the long run. He was very talented and, in certain ways, politically skillful, so he was able to land on his feet. He simply went to another job. But my behavior hurt me!

On several occasions I tried earnestly to help him. Specifically, I tried to get him to modify his actions so that he would stop alienating people. One night I stayed at the job until nine or ten—when I should have been home with my family—attempting to assure him, coach him, and so on. What a waste! What a mistake!

He did not want coaching or reassurance. To be absolutely candid, he really had no commitment to staying in that work setting anyway. I did. I believed that there was much good to be done and that both of us should stay there and do it. My own needs and wishes caused me *not* to see the obvious fact that, no matter what he said, *he did not want to.*

Be wise in choosing whom you try to rescue. Your time and energy are important. Once they are spent, you do not get them back in this life. Ask yourself *why* others are foundering in the middle of the ocean without a life preserver. What did they do, or not do, to get thrown overboard? Do they want to be rescued? What exactly will it cost you?

Whom, if anyone, are you currently trying to help?
Are you spending your time and energy wisely in these helping efforts?
Are there ways, other than helping, in which you are giving away your
    resources and, if so, are these good expenditures?

SELF-EVALUATION RATING: 1   2   3   4   5

NOTES AND REFLECTIONS:

GUIDELINE 13

A simple man believes every word he hears; a clever man understands the need for proof (Proverbs 14:15, NEB).

Imagine that your favorite news commentator announces that a medical researcher has discovered that cancer patients have an unusually low level of a certain vitamin in their bodies. This researcher, we are told, has repeated these measurements at several hospitals across the country. The results have been verified consistently. *Time* is going to run the discovery as its cover story. What would happen?

People who have cancer, or who fear that they might, would probably run out to buy a lot of vitamin supplements.

Unfortunately there would be a major problem with all of this. Even if cancer patients do show a vitamin deficiency, this does NOT prove that the deficiency caused the cancer! Both cancer and the dearth of the vitamin could have been caused by some third thing, yet to be discovered.

You could argue that, were there only a one percent chance that the vitamin prevents or cures cancer, it is well worth taking the supplements. This might be true, unless of course there was a medical reason not to take them. The point remains that most people would be unable or unwilling to reason this all out. Let me offer two more brief examples:

CLAIM: Bigger cars are safer because there are fewer fatalities in luxury cars.

RESPONSE: Yes, but older people drive the luxury cars because, as a rule, only they can afford them. The little cars are more often driven by young people who, clearly, take more unnecessary risks. (Large cars probably *are* safer, but the effects of who drives what have to be taken into consideration.)

CLAIM: More ice cream is sold in the summertime, which is also when more people drown. Obviously, eating ice cream causes people to drown.

RESPONSE: You've got to be kidding!

Most of us are gullible in one way or another. Some people are quick to believe hot tips. Others readily believe certain kinds of news stories. Still others are easily conned by salespersons. Education is supposed to build into us some healthy doubt, and to some extent it does. Well-educated people are usually less likely to believe something just because it is in print or because some famous person says it. Yet we all have psychological needs to believe certain kinds of things. What we need to believe may differ greatly from what the person next to us needs to believe.

If the orb in which you function is a relatively sophisticated one, what you can afford to accept as "proof" becomes critical. Within some business settings, for example, the claims are made by highly intelligent people. They may or may not be honest, but they are routinely able, impressive, and believable. Sometimes they are mostly slick and self-serving, and you can act on what they say only at your own peril.

Weigh carefully what others claim. Although you cannot function well from a paranoid position, it is important to exercise a bit of appropriate wariness. Human motives can be exceedingly complex. Always ask yourself what the potential payoff might be to the person making a claim if you believed and acted on it. Even the best of people can have bad motives now and then.

In what specific areas, if any, do you tend to "believe" too quickly?
What sorts of claims are you most predisposed to accept?
Toward which individuals might you wisely exercise more discretionary caution?

SELF-EVALUATION RATING: 1   2   3   4   5

NOTES AND REFLECTIONS:

GOING ALL OUT

Hard work always yields its profit, idle talk brings only want (Proverbs 14:23, JB); The lazy hunter puts up no game, but the industrious man reaps a rich harvest (Proverbs 12:27, NEB).

There are few shortcuts to success. Although some people work hard and still do not succeed, very few of us ever succeed without working hard. Some highly successful people, who have actually almost killed themselves to achieve what they have, make it appear that they never strained harder than to sign autographs or endorse checks. There is great poise, and perhaps great art, to making the difficult look easy. The rock-hard truth, however, is that few actresses are "discovered" on the Malibu beach, few corporation presidents coast their way to the top, and few millionaires acquire their wealth by throwing darts at the business section of the newspaper.

The most obvious reason for avoiding hard work is that it can be painful. Just about no one likes to put in fourteen-hour days—except, of course, workaholics who stay at the office so that they do not have to go home. Unless work is your way of avoiding something, it takes a lot of discipline to stay at it after your eyes start burning and your back aches. It is so much more appealing to sit in front of the television or to crawl into bed. The people who win Nobel Prizes forgo these pleasures. In psychological jargon, they "delay gratification." If you want to achieve, you have to be willing to put in effort and, sometimes, to put up with pain.

Usually you also have to do this over a long period of time. For work to succeed it typically has to be consistent. This is what the "Tortoise and Hare" story is about. To read a long book, you have to keep at it, sometimes to read every chance you get, page after page, chapter after chapter. Large houses are built from many bricks.

People refuse to work hard for reasons other than a lack of fortitude or endurance. Some people consider hard work the backbone of our civilization; others regard it as the royal road to the coronary care unit. Some people lust for fame and fortune; others are contented with being an ordinary person. Some people are willing to split their loyalties between work and family, or even to sacrifice the latter for the former; others do not want to deprive themselves or their loved ones of even one minute they could spend together. A person who clearly understands the high price of success, refuses to pay it, and then accepts the consequences is probably in pretty good psychological shape. Such a person is wisely "counting the cost" before signing the contract. But some of us shy away from hard work for reasons less healthy.

When I was in college I would sometimes not study for an examination until the night before I had to take it. If I got an "A," I was able to congratulate myself for being so smart. If I earned a lesser grade, I could say to myself, "Why, of course. I didn't have enough time to study." By doing this sort of thing, I was able to preserve my image of myself as quite a clever fellow, no matter what. Although I would not have admitted it at the time, I was actually afraid of failure.

As the author of the first proverb seems to suggest, some of us use talking as a substitute for acting. Words serve some truly incredible psychological functions, among them the creating of illusions. We can use words as vehicles of magic. For example, by making endless lists of what we intend to do, we can avoid ever doing anything. By "talking a good game" in the business world, we can endlessly put off ever actually having to play.

It is very important to review your words-to-work ratio from time to time, to make sure that you are not fooling yourself. Taking inventory once in a while can help keep you on the track in which you desire to travel.

Are you clear about your professional goals, and about how these relate to your other goals?
Are you putting in enough effort to achieve what you intend?
Are you backing away from all-out effort because you fear failure?
Are there areas in which you use words as a magical substitute for work?

SELF-EVALUATION RATING: 1   2   3   4   5

NOTES AND REFLECTIONS:

49

GUIDELINE 15

Diligence brings a man to power (Proverbs 12:24, NEB).

The world is full of people who are in positions of major responsibility because they proved trustworthy. They did their homework as well as their best. As they demonstrated that they could do one thing effectively, often through being willing to put in a little extra effort, they were asked to do something more significant. In this fashion, they ascended their particular occupational ladders, rung by rung.

A friend of mine began working years ago in a small Sunbelt bank. His starting position was modest, but he was soon promoted to a post of more importance. Within a couple of years, he was getting offers from other banks. Not long after that he accepted a position in the San Francisco office of one of the largest financial institutions in the country. He continued to do well and was promoted, again and again.

Eventually, he "retired" from this institution. Taking the money he had accumulated, he set about multiplying it. This too he did with great success. I have never been brash enough to ask him to tell me his net worth, but I can assure you that it is substantial.

"How did you do it?" I asked. "You're still a young man."

"When I worked for the banks," he said, "I would always work a little harder than everyone else. I always did a little extra, stayed just a little ahead. When one of the senior vice-presidents would ask me to do something, I would quietly agree and promise to have it done within a week or two. Most of the time I had it done already, sitting in my desk drawer. I'd just wait a couple days and then deliver it. I was usually even able to beat out the Harvard M.B.A.'s. I've done the same thing with my investments. I just work hard."

Actually, I think it would be more accurate to say that he worked diligently. Diligence denotes not only hard work but a certain carefulness, in other words, attention to detail.

Working harder does not necessarily mean working smarter. Neither does getting lost in details. I have seen more than one corporation executive in trouble because he could not see the bigger picture and delegate certain kinds of tasks to others. Nevertheless, careful and consistent effort is normally a prerequisite to getting promoted or capturing a larger share of a market, both of which can be viewed as an increase in power.

Power is an elusive object of study. It is not tangible, like a poker chip or a bank note. Power is more the constantly changing capacity to get your way, to influence others. There is, of course, formal and informal power —what the organizational chart says and what is really true. A person's power can rise or fall dramatically on the strength of one decision.

As I noted in the Introduction, some writers regard power as an end in itself, which I argued was shortsighted. Power is better thought of as a means. It enables you to achieve things, good or bad. Although power can corrupt, it can also be used for great good. If you are a decent person— and you probably would never have opened this book if you were not— you might as well wield as much power as you can. Otherwise, someone far less decent may do the job instead. Do be careful however. Power has turned some otherwise good human beings into real monsters.

Diligently serve those around you and you will almost certainly be entrusted with some kind of power. If you already have power, you will probably be given more!

In what areas could you serve more diligently?
At this time in your career, how do you regard power?

SELF-EVALUATION RATING: 1   2   3   4   5

NOTES AND REFLECTIONS:

Schemes lightly made come to nothing, but with long planning they succeed (Proverbs 15:22, NEB).

J. R. R. Tolkien worked on his *Lord of the Rings* trilogy for many years before he submitted it for publication. Tolkien was not in a hurry. An accomplished scholar, he knew how long it usually takes to turn out something that is truly first-rate. His close attention to plot, character, and, most of all, language yielded its rewards. Besides whatever fame and fortune these books bestowed on their author, they represent a lasting contribution to Western literature.

Such painstaking effort runs counter to some of our most cherished values. The majority of people are impressed more with speed than with care. By definition, however, great business leaders are in the minority, and their attitudes show it. They are often known for their careful planning.

For several years, a good friend and I have been meeting for breakfast every few weeks to discuss, among other things, possible business ventures. We have considered hundreds of ideas, some of them promising. Whenever we come up with what I consider to be a "winner," I almost always want to get on with it immediately. He, on the other hand, presses for more reflection, more planning. Being a wise man with much corporate savvy, he does this gently and always reinforces me for my creativity. Yet, in his wisdom, he understands that the difference between success and failure often hinges on *thought.* A few months ago, by the way, he finally said: "This may be it. I think we've really got something here." I'm glad I hung in there!

Sometimes the shortest distance to a goal is NOT a beeline. The core issue here is real versus illusory efficiency. By rushing around doing lots of irrelevant work, you can convince yourself that you are accomplishing something when, in fact, you are only tiring yourself out. We have just so much time, energy, and capital. Squandering these resources by spending them prematurely is like shooting off all your fireworks the day before the celebration. When the right time comes, you have nothing left.

Samurai warriors were notorious for their efficiency. Economy of effort was the hallmark of their skill. Every shift of the body, every move of the sword was purposeful. Nothing wasted, nothing random. What Westerners tend to miss about the Samurai is that their minds were trained for battle every bit as much as their bodies were.

They were trained to *think* in a way that made their actions literally afterthoughts. Effective business people are, in this way, like Samurai. Their major battlefields lie within the territories of their minds. What they actually do is just the concrete expression of this battle. Unfortunately most of us join the battle on the wrong field, whether this is the board room, the golf course, or the negotiation table.

If you want to do your best, you have to sit down with that ugly yellow pad and start scribbling. Make lists, draw boxes, draft flow charts, construct graphs. Sometimes the most beneficial thing you can do is just to sit there with the pad on your lap and do nothing but think. I have been amazed at how reluctant people are to do this, lest they waste time. Like some animals separated from food by a glass barrier, they hopelessly try to push through instead of walk around it.

What are the benefits of planning? First, you can see problems coming and work out solutions in advance. Second, you can better evaluate the true merits and demerits of your various alternatives. Third, you make yourself more likely to consult others who can help you gain perspective (the RSV translates this proverb as, "Without counsel plans go wrong, but with many advisers they succeed"). Fourth, and most important, you do not run away from work by running into it. Don't be one of those persons who are working so hard that they can't make any money.

As much as you can, run your work life as the Samurai fought their battles: in the mind.

How much do you tend to run away from uncertainty, and the tension it brings, by poorly guided flights into action?

Is there something about which you need to do more thinking before you take further action?

SELF-EVALUATION RATING: 1   2   3   4   5

NOTES AND REFLECTIONS:

GUIDELINE 17

Wealth hastily gotten will dwindle, but he who gathers little by little will increase it (Proverbs 13:11, RSV).

Whether a particular person moves in the direction of accumulating wealth seems to depend a great deal on his or her economic habits. Does the person save or spend? Take intelligent risks or play irrational long shots?

Such economic habits are often greatly affected by how quickly one acquires financial resources. Have they come all at once, perhaps the result of winning the Irish Sweepstakes? Or, have they come through years of consistent and painstaking effort? One's experiences condition one's attitudes which, in turn, set the stage for one's future behavior. The proverb writer is contrasting the likely attitudes of the person who, step by step, accumulates resources versus those of the person who has perhaps had a windfall profit.

To do almost anything well requires discipline. People who suddenly come into money typically underestimate the amount of WORK that goes into the proper care of wealth. This is why the news often carries stories of persons who have tragically squandered inheritances or who, having made a financial killing, immediately turn around and lose their entire fortunes.

Those who increase and hold on to their gains have learned to save, to sacrifice, to scrutinize carefully their own financial actions. Through years of practice, most have developed good economic attitudes and habits. Successful accumulators seem to share a number of characteristics:

First, they tend to view the accumulation of resources as a way of life, not a temporary blitzkrieg. From my clinical practice, I know that people who attempt to lose weight through fad diets usually fail. If they do lose a few pounds, they are almost certain to gain them back within a short time. On the other hand, people who change their basic habits and attitudes *do* accomplish their weight-control goals. For example, they learn to eat more slowly, to monitor conscientiously their caloric intakes, to resist making social occasions out of meals, to develop substitute behaviors for running to the refrigerator, and so on.

Similarly, people who amass wealth learn to indulge less frequently, to spend less lavishly, to resist the acquisition of trendy gimmicks and questionable gadgets, to refuse the use of credit for consumption (but not necessarily for investment leverage), to abstain from joining frivolous crazes. Perhaps most important of all, successful accumulators keep and periodically review records of everything they spend. This can be an enlightening and painful process. It is hard to admit one's economic sins!

Second, effective accumulators tend to reinvest the yields from previously successful investments. They do not take profits only to go on spending sprees. Some investment counselors speak of this as "not eating one's monetary children." Good investors have the progressive mentality of that legendary mathematician who, when asked by the caliph what he wanted as payment for counting the ruler's armies, replied, "One grain of wheat for the first square on the chessboard, two grains for the second square, four for the third, eight for the fourth . . ."

Third, despite their relentless movement in the direction of accumulation, the economically successful are characteristically NOT stingy or cheap. They know, for example, that it is not worth the loss of others' respect and goodwill to get hung up on whether a dinner check has been divided precisely. Their images are worth far more than a dollar or two. They also do not wait for a good investment to come down a few cents before they buy or, alternatively, for their profits to go up a few cents before they sell. They are not "penny wise and dollar foolish."

There is another dimension to this proverb that is worth noting. Some translations of "wealth hastily gotten" imply "that which one has acquired dishonorably." If one fails to learn good economic ways through windfall profits, how much prudence can one expect to learn through theft? Con men do not make good investment fund managers, even when they are managing their own funds.

If you want the blessings of wealth, proceed with determination, discipline, and honor.

Are you financially persistent?
Do you exercise sufficient economic discipline?

SELF-EVALUATION RATING: 1   2   3   4   5

NOTES AND REFLECTIONS:

WISDOM OF THE TONGUE

GUIDELINE 18

The lips of the righteous know what is fitting, but the mouth of the wicked only what is perverse (Proverbs 10:32, NIV).

Goodness, or what the Bible terms righteousness, is closely related to graciousness. Good-hearted people are gracious people. They are positive, considerate, loving.

Some people, however, always seem to see the negative. They are critical and inflexible. Unlike people who extend themselves to say things that are appropriate and constructive, they carp, grouse, and complain without regard for what this does to others.

The author of the proverb seems to be saying that good people care enough about *others* to say the right things, while bad people care only about discharging their venomous spleens. The latter are rigidly locked into "perverse" talk. Another translation (NEB) renders this as "subversive talk." The proverb writer is contrasting the person who knows and says what is fitting with the person who chronically foments malice.

How does one always say the socially fitting thing without becoming a Pollyanna or a hypocrite? What if someone or something *is* truly terrible, even evil?

Suppose the boss ruthlessly and without cause fires someone who has five young children to support.

Suppose everyone around you is viciously picking on the new kid just for the sport of it.

Suppose the person on whom you rely most directly openly sabotages you.

This proverb is not advocating passivity. There are times when the worst thing you could do would be to keep your mouth shut.

"Mr. Martin, I would like to ask you if you could possibly consider reinstating Jim Hill. I'd be glad to work with him to make sure that he does his job exactly the way you want. Maybe I could give him a little time each night after we close."

"Come on, you guys have had your fun. Leave the kid alone. Give him a few months to get to know us before you roast him."

"John, come in here. I need to speak with you privately. You've worked for me for a long time now. Is it true that you . . . ?"

These are *good* things to say. They are tactful, yet strong. Such statements can also involve risk to you. Mr. Martin may tell you to follow Hill out the door. The mob may turn on you as well as the kid. Your subordinate may sabotage you all the more violently in the future for daring to bring up the matter. Nonetheless, the best thing to do in each case is probably to speak up when the time seems right.

Many people opportunistically use just about any occasion that comes along to express their own anger and bitterness. At issue is whether we can respond to what is in front of us—to reality. Can we speak and act in a way that "fits" what is going on, or are we stuck in the groove of character assassination? Can we rise above negativity or are we doomed to inject it into everything, to make it part of our life script?

The person who penned this proverb seems to be telling us that one route to more effective social behavior is goodness. If your heart is pure, your actions will be "fitting." Since others reward us, in business and elsewhere, for appropriate social behavior, goodness has its practical advantages. However much negative talk may please people at the moment, no one likes or trusts a rigidly critical person. This is because people sense, usually correctly, that they could quickly become targets of criticism.

To function at your best, inspire in others the confidence that you can be trusted NOT to use them as targets. Keep your heart pure and your speech gracious.

How appropriate have your words been during the past several days?
How given are you to subversive talk?
What, if anything, triggers unproductive negativity in you and how might you avoid getting caught up in destructive talk?

SELF-EVALUATION RATING: 1   2   3   4   5

NOTES AND REFLECTIONS:

GUIDELINE 19

Don't talk so much. You keep putting your foot in your mouth. Be sensible and turn off the flow (Proverbs 10:19, TLB).

Deep within the brain, there is a set of neural structures that, together, are known as the limbic system. This system of interacting brain structures seems to be the seat of human emotionality. When certain parts of the limbic system are overstimulated, we have strong feelings, ranging from rage to terror.

One way to overactivate your limbic system is to talk too much, which is perhaps why we use the expression "to keep one's peace" in connection with being quiet. Once these emotional centers are overactivated we tend to talk all the more. In this way, a vicious circle can be set off by jumping into conversation too quickly. While there is nothing wrong with emotions per se, and certainly nothing wrong with talking, overly intense emotional states can prompt us to say imprudent things. What we say can become convoluted, complex.

As a psychotherapist I have learned to be wary of too much complexity in human affairs. When things become overly complicated, something unwholesome is usually going on. People do not do their best when they are running in different directions at the same time, or when they are simply moving about randomly, without a clear purpose. Because we are, by nature, both thinking and feeling beings, it is important that we balance the cognitive and emotional sides of ourselves. We need to *experience* our feelings without acting on every one of them. Talking too much makes us more vulnerable to emotional and behavioral chaos.

The crucial thing to avoid is making public statements to work out your private problems. People who talk too much are almost always trying to reduce their own inner tensions, to resolve mental conflicts. Reducing tensions and resolving conflicts are desirable, but the price for doing this via committee meetings or sales conferences is much too high. It would be better to talk to yourself in the mirror!

Another translation of this proverb (NEB) renders it as, "When men talk too much, sin is never far away; common sense holds its tongue." Note that, while other proverbs deal with the undesirability of gossip, this one concerns the relationship between talk and action within the individual. Somehow, excessive talk makes us more likely to "sin." An ancient way of understanding sin is missing the mark. The distance between the bull's-eye of an archer's target and his arrow was called "sin." We are more likely to miss the mark when we compulsively talk.

Psychologists who specialize in the study of learning speak of "response latency." By this they mean the time it takes a person or an animal to react to something. When we talk too much, we usually have *short* latencies. Instead of counting to three before we speak, we rush in—sometimes where even angels would not!

If you tend at times to say more than you should, there are a few things you can do that may help. First, do not let yourself talk until you feel that you have the necessary composure. Try to interrupt the limbic-tongue "reflex." Regard the buildup of tension as a sign that you probably should WAIT, especially if you are prone to use public conversation to reduce this tension. Second, work on increasing your response latencies. Begin by keeping track of how long it usually takes you to respond to what someone else says. One second? Two seconds? Three? Try to add a second a week to your latencies, until you get them where you believe they should be. Third, use short sentences and paragraphs. Measure your words. Concentrate on saying what you have to say with style. Fourth, if you need to lower your emotional reactivity in meetings, you might try taking along something to drain off some of your attention, for example, some paper work. Make sure that you do this only if you can do so unobtrusively, without offending others.

In which specific situations, if any, do you tend to talk too much?
If you do talk more than you would like, what concrete things could you do to inhibit your impulses to speak?

SELF-EVALUATION RATING: 1   2   3   4   5

NOTES AND REFLECTIONS:

GUIDELINE 20

Be in no hurry to tell everyone what you have seen, or it will end in bitter reproaches from your friend (Proverbs 25:8, NEB).

During the first few years of my psychological practice, I felt a responsibility to tell the client everything that I discovered, as soon as I discovered it. Like many other young therapists, I had to learn that good clinicians bide their time, waiting for the moment when the client is *ready* to hear. The therapist can have all kinds of insights, but these will prove of very limited value until the client is capable of absorbing them.

Most of us have considerable trouble accepting certain truths about ourselves. Who wants to be told unflattering things? We sometimes find such information incredibly painful. Too much truth at one time overwhelms us and raises our defenses. It makes us feel threatened and helpless and, thus, usually angry.

In my personal as well as my professional life, I have struggled a great deal with the issue of self-disclosure. Many people, particularly in competitive environments, reveal almost nothing about themselves, lest it be used against them. They hide, they rationalize, they do almost anything they can to make you think only the best of them. This always seemed spineless to me. Perhaps in reaction to such close-to-the-vest playing, I decided that withholding any information was always dishonest. I now see that this is not necessarily so.

People have just so much tolerance for confrontation. If we go around saying everything we think or feel, we will earn "bitter reproaches" even from our friends.

I suppose this proverb is also warning us against carrying tales. Few people like the bearer of bad tidings, which is why we hear talk of "slain messengers." A manager, despite temporary shows of interest, may not really WANT to know about the misdeeds of his or her employees. A husband or wife, similarly, may not want to know about the misconduct of a spouse. A parent may not want to hear that his or her child has misbehaved. Information can have powerful effects that are not always desirable. Naturally, there are times when it is right to deliver information, quite aside from whether the other person wants to hear it, but it takes good judgment to recognize when such times are upon us.

Not to say something when we feel the urge is to have to carry it around inside. It is sometimes difficult to do this, to "live in one's own head." Personally I would much rather tell others what I think and feel, especially when it is about them, than to reflect quietly by myself. I *want* to communicate. Contrary to a lot of mental health mythology, however, communication is not always desirable. Sometimes all it does is to inflict pain.

Truly wise people know what to say and when. Like good athletes, they know the value of TIMING. The right thing said at the wrong time can result in absolute disaster. Because they choose their words carefully, what they say is usually beneficial to others. It is also beneficial to them, since they do not sacrifice their relationships on the altars of verbal foolishness.

Watch. Listen. Reflect. As much as you can, become a keen observer. Attend especially to the *sequences* in which things are said by different people. Draw your conclusions and, if they are negative, weigh carefully whether stating them is likely to do any good. What might it cost you to say what you are thinking? Of course, when you are pitting your integrity against your safety, the decision can only be made by you. In the contemporary business world—and perhaps it has always been so—safety tends to prevail over integrity far too often.

When, and to which specific people, are you likely to say too much?
When you are about to say something that the other person will find painful, do you focus more on his or her welfare or on your own need to talk?

SELF-EVALUATION RATING: 1   2   3   4   5

NOTES AND REFLECTIONS:

GUIDELINE 21

Do not speak in the hearing of a fool, for he will despise the wisdom of your words (Proverbs 23:9, RSV).

To talk with someone is to make an investment. Each of us has only a finite amount of time on earth and we can spend time conversing with only a relatively small number of people. When you talk with someone, you *spend* part of your life.

Let me make this a little more concrete. In the typical human life, there are somewhere between 25,000 and 35,000 days. Within the ordinary work year, there are between 2,000 and 2,500 hours. A week consists of 168 hours, of which we sleep 60 to 70, leaving roughly 100 hours for everything else. Clearly, contrary to what we think when we are very young, a lifetime does not last forever. Ultimately, there is no such thing as "free time." Any time we use, we pay for dearly, since—as far as we know—it never comes again.

This proverb says, in essence, spend your time wisely. Make good interpersonal investments. Again contrary to a lot of ridiculous rhetoric, everyone is not equally worthy of one's time. The writer seems to be saying, "Don't waste your time." Investing your time and energy in someone who lacks either the capacity or the will to learn is, indeed, to waste some of your life.

As I write this, I think of all the people in my life who get mad at me because I do not give them as much of my time as they would like. Perhaps I should feel flattered, and I think I remember that once I wanted to be sought after this way. Mostly, though, I just resent their anger.

It is *my* life. God has given it to me as a sacred trust account, to manage according to my best judgment. It is my job to be the wisest trustee of this account that I can, not to surrender blindly its management to others. No matter what, we should spend our lives in the way that we think he wants us to, even if this offends the whole world!

But the author of the proverb is also getting at something else. He is advising us to "watch what we say around foolish people." Saying the wrong thing to someone who might mindlessly repeat it is surely to ask for trouble. Saying the right thing to someone who does not have the sense to appreciate it is only to court pain.

Sometimes our own good-heartedness outweighs our good sense. At least this is the case with me. While I have always been extremely careful about protecting the confidences of others, I have not always been so careful to protect my own. For example, I have occasionally shared information about myself that, later, I was sorry I had. My intent was to help the other person. My reward was only to suffer. For the sake of perspective, I should add that, on sum, personal sharing has been more of a blessing than a curse, but the point of the proverb remains: use good judgment in what you say to whom. As Francis Bacon suggested, "Knowledge is power." To give others knowledge about you is often to give them power over you.

Another translation (NEB) renders the first part of this proverb: "Hold your tongue in the hearing of a stupid man." Perhaps the love of wisdom is a kind of intelligence all its own, while a distaste for wisdom, even in a technical genius, is a singular kind of stupidity. If so, the challenge of this proverb is to be able to distinguish among the different types of intelligence. The whiz kid down the hall who earned his M.B.A. from Stanford at twenty-one and who can do regression equations in his sleep may not have much of an aptitude for wisdom!

Protect yourself. Spend your time and energy wisely. Remember the statement from the New Testament: "Do not throw your pearls before swine."

Are you spending your life wisely, or wasting parts of it in unfruitful conversations?

Are you sharing confidences with the right people?

Are there particular people who seem to draw you into saying more than you should and, if so, how might you stop this? (Hints: "Let me think that one through before I give you my opinion." "I'd prefer not to comment —if I did, I wouldn't feel right." "That's an interesting question . . . [purposeful silence].")

SELF-EVALUATION RATING: 1   2   3   4   5

NOTES AND REFLECTIONS:

GUIDELINE 22

Even a fool, if he holds his peace, is thought wise; keep your mouth shut and show your good sense (Proverbs 17:28, NEB).

Shortly after I entered college, I attended a party in New York City. It was hosted by my prep school senior English teacher, who had invited several of his old friends: psychoanalysts, artists, and so on. One of his guests was a clean-cut man of about fifty, who as I recall won a prestigious architectural prize when he was a student at Yale. He was intelligent, urbane, and *wise.* It did not take long for us to become immersed in intense conversation, because I very much wanted to learn everything I could from him.

I clearly remember him saying: "If you enter a room full of strangers and simply keep your mouth shut, people will imagine all the wonderful things about you they want. Once you start talking, you begin to dismantle their grand illusions." A related Confucian proverb states, "Better to be thought a fool than open one's mouth and confirm it."

Lying low or "cutting a low profile," as it is called, is sometimes a magnificently effective way to enhance your prestige. Perhaps other people need so much to talk that they are grateful to you for giving them a chance, and so they reward you by thinking well of you. Perhaps just about everyone wants to have heroes and heroines, so that all you have to do is provide them with a blank screen and they will "project" onto you heroic qualities. Whatever the psychological mechanisms underlying the benefits of lying low, these benefits *can* be considerable. For one thing, being quiet gives you the chance to listen. And as I have suggested, you enhance your image of sagacity and, thus, your persuasive influence.

I do want to add some twentieth-century qualifications that derive from social psychology. First, you cannot expect endless silence to make you look like Einstein. At least once in a while, you have to say *something* intelligent. However, a porpoise could probably meet this requirement, just by choosing wisely from among the possible things it might think of to say. Again, if you speak sparingly and thus treat what others say with attentive respect; they will naturally evaluate what you do say in a favorable light. The whole thing is a little bit like money and inflation. When there's too much money—or talk—its value goes down.

Second, some research suggests that people who talk more are generally assumed to be more competent than those who talk less. From carefully watching others through years of committee meetings, I have come to the informal conclusion that the key issue is not quantity of speech but dominance. People who talk more tend to be more dominant, and it is dominance (assertiveness) that prompts others to think of one as competent. Some people who talk a great deal are known by everyone to be blowhards, not to be trusted with bundling last week's newspapers.

Probably there is a trade-off between dominance and quiet. Both, if not overdone, have their merits. The ultimate ideal would be quiet strength, that is, positioning yourself so that, on those rare occasions when you speak, others listen. If you are too dominant, others will resent you. Although they may automatically perceive you as generally more competent, they may no longer entertain all those wonderful fantasies about you that silence can usher in. This may prove a critical loss. What you say and how you say it DOES count. Others take off for mistakes.

The proverb we are considering is really saying something like this: If you do not know what you're talking about, keep quiet and let others spin their wonderful fantasies of you. If you do know what you're talking about, and they are ready to listen, perhaps you should take the risk of saying what you think.

Do you maintain your silent poise, or do you tend to destroy the good things others might think of you by talking too readily?

In what specific situations, and with which specific people, do you tend most to lose your silent poise?

SELF-EVALUATION RATING: 1   2   3   4   5

NOTES AND REFLECTIONS:

WHEN MODESTY HELPS

GUIDELINE 23

Better to be a nobody and yet have a servant than pretend to be somebody and have no food (Proverbs 12:9, NIV).

All of us know people who are quite simply obnoxious in their arrogance. They communicate that they should be served, that others are beneath them, that they are too good to do what they expect the rest of us to be willing to do, whether it is to take minutes, make calls, or empty ashtrays. Such persons are not usually popular. Others see them as offensively proud and pretentious.

Most human endeavors operate on the basis of social relationships. It is a common misconception about business, for example, that what matters most to everyone is the bottom line. Profit is presumed to be everything. Surely businesses need to be profitable in order to sustain themselves, but profit—money—is sometimes only a *symbol.* Money, while not of itself everything, tends to be taken as an index of what ultimately *does* matter to nearly all of us: how we feel about ourselves.

People may tell you that they are working for a larger home, a bigger share of the company, even a luxurious yacht. Although such claims may be true, they by no means account for how hard most of us work.

We all want to value ourselves, to enjoy the esteem of ourselves and others (the latter is usually called status). When you act in an arrogant way, you put others down and, in the process, take away from their esteem. Sometimes when others see us as bragging, we are intending merely to express our confidence, to share our joy, to delight in our own achievements and capacities—quite aside from how they compare with anyone else's. Yet such behavior can raise others' anxieties, depress them, and make them feel comparatively worthless and inadequate.

Let me be frank. Out of my own natural enthusiasm I tend at times to act expansively. Occasionally I notice that, instead of joining in my celebrations, others pull back. Sometimes they look overtly despondent! I have had to remind myself to consider the effects of my self-congratulations on them and to admit that others may genuinely experience my innocent boasts as a subtle form of hostile dominance. To them, the message that comes through, intended or not, is: "I am better than you are."

This proverb is warning us that there can be serious consequences to pretense, perhaps even when we do not intend to be pretentious. We can lose our jobs. Arrogance and pretentiousness may not be exactly the same, but they often go together.

Another translation (NEB) of this proverb is: "It is better to be modest and earn one's living than to be conceited and go hungry." We could just as well substitute the word "inflated" for conceited. Thus the proverb would read, "It is better to be modest and earn one's living than to be *inflated* and go hungry." Our inflations are usually others' deflations. Some recent psychological research has supported the idea that a little modesty does indeed make us more attractive to others.

Naturally, there are qualifications. Too much modesty makes you look incompetent, like an obsequious buffoon. Another line of research has demonstrated, for example, that a blunder by a public figure, say, a politician or a scientist, will make the audience like him or her more . . . but only if they previously regarded this figure as clearly possessing lots of status. For the president of the company to spill coffee on himself may help him or her seem more human, more approachable. For the junior executive to spill coffee may only make him or her seem clumsy. Pratfalls, as they are called, seem to help only if you have a substantial edge already. Modesty is like that. It has to be evident in the appropriate doses.

If you tend to be more expansive about your own achievements and abilities than you should be, adjust your self-presentation so that you are less likely to offend others. On the other hand, don't go too far in the opposite direction either!

How modest do you tend to be?
Are there particular circumstances in which you tend to be too expansive?
Are there particular people whose feelings you may be hurting, just by telling them how well things are going for you?
Are you hurting your reputation, or your chances for advancement, by too often blowing your own horn?

SELF-EVALUATION RATING: 1   2   3   4   5

NOTES AND REFLECTIONS:

GUIDELINE 24

A fool thinks that he is always right (Proverbs 12:15, NEB); A clever man conceals his knowledge, but a stupid man broadcasts his folly (Proverbs 12:23, NEB).

"My mind is already made up; don't confuse me with the facts!" This is the attitude that the first proverb seems to be warning against. All of us have had the experience of trying to get others to listen when they just did not want to hear. They "knew what was what," and there was little chance of getting them to change their opinions.

Sometimes the people who are the least well informed speak the loudest and with the most conviction. They support their own illusions with sheer passion. "I must be right. Can't you hear how loud I'm speaking?"

I have seen at least one person's career ruined because he so strongly maintained, and loudly broadcast, opinions that were plainly silly to everyone else. It seemed that the more foolish the opinion, the more vehemently he held it. Eventually, he developed a reputation for incompetence. At that point, even if he had won the Pulitzer Prize it would not have helped. I felt sorry for him. He was his own worst enemy.

Why do we sometimes close our minds? What is it that impels us sometimes to talk the most when we know the least?

Psychologists who study perception—how we see, hear, and so on—speak of the principle of closure. By this they mean that we all have a natural tendency to finish whatever is incomplete. Thus, for example, if we see a circle or a square with a piece missing, we have an almost irresistible urge to fill in the missing piece. Even if we do not take out a pencil, we complete the figure in our minds. We want things to be complete, neatly tied up, no loose strings hanging about and, most of all, no missing parts!

Intelligence is, in part, the ability to *resist* premature closure, that is, the capacity to wait until one has sufficiently analyzed a problem before drawing conclusions. A great deal of research has demonstrated, for example, that people who get fixated do not make good problem solvers. Their thinking is too rigid, too conventional. Interestingly, intellectual rigidity tends to increase with anxiety. In general, the more threatened we feel, the less flexible our thinking and the more we tend to close our minds. To think well, we have to stay loose.

Anxiety also seems to lie at the root of our tendency to "broadcast our folly." George Santayana once said that a fanatic is someone who, having lost sight of his purpose, redoubles his efforts. We are all a little like that. When we begin to wonder if we really know something, especially when this something is important to us, we often try all the harder to convince ourselves that we do. One way we do this is to hold forth more intensely. Instead of facing our uncertainties, we attempt to obliterate them through a magical will to believe.

Another line of research suggests that we tend to justify our past actions. We do not like to be inconsistent. We like our behaviors and beliefs to line up nicely. Hence, we will argue vehemently for principles that are in accord with what we have already done, even if it is obvious to everyone else that what we did was a mistake. We are most in danger of "broadcasting our folly" when we have already done something foolish!

Now, about the wisdom of concealing our knowledge: The proverb writer is *not* telling us to hoard knowledge, refusing to give it to others when they can profit from it. He is, however, telling us to err on the side of understatement rather than overstatement. He is advising us to exercise some judgment about what we say when, instead of spilling our intellectual guts at every turn.

The second proverb could be taken to mean, "People who talk a lot cannot possibly know what they are talking about, since those who truly know do not talk!"

How much do you tend to compound your errors by publicly justifying your past mistakes?
Are there particular subjects on which you tend quickly to close your mind?
In which situations, if any, do you too readily broadcast knowledge? Folly?
Are you generally able to determine when and when not to speak (see Ecclesiastes 3)?

SELF-EVALUATION RATING: 1   2   3   4   5

NOTES AND REFLECTIONS:

GUIDELINE 25

Poverty and disgrace come to him who ignores instruction, but he who heeds reproof is honored (Proverbs 13:18, RSV); The way to honour is humility (Proverbs 15:33b, NEB).

Few of us like to be brought up short. There is just something about us that makes us bristle under criticism. Our tendency is to fight back, to discount what is being said to us, to justify ourselves. Often, as a defense, we impugn the motives or the competence of the person criticizing us. Yet as another translation (NEB) of the first proverb warns, "To refuse correction brings poverty and contempt." Our resistance to learning from others' criticisms, regardless of whether these "others" are friends or foes, can hurt our financial well-being as well as our social standing.

In my work as a psychotherapist, I can often estimate pretty well during the first interview how much a new client is likely to profit from psychological help. Intelligence helps. Clients who are bright are more able to grasp psychological subtleties. Anxiety helps. Clients who are in acute misery are usually more motivated to work. Optimism helps. Clients who expect things to get better and to accomplish something in therapy typically have the endurance to stick with the process when it becomes painful. What seems to help most of all, however, is the willingness to learn. The people who best learn life's lessons are those who have the humility to accept its teachings.

I have had the good fortune to get to know several top executives in diverse industries. What amazes me about them is that they seem so open to criticism. They are not by any means weak or indecisive, nor are they gluttons for punishment. As a matter of fact, as a group they are strong, decisive, and tough. But they are also genuinely willing to examine themselves. To them, criticism is by definition constructive, if only for the reason that it prompts them to think about something they might have ignored. It does not matter to them whether the person delivering the criticism is smart or stupid, loving or hateful. What does matter is the *opportunity* carried on the wings of any critique. Like successful people in any endeavor, they know how to turn potential liabilities into actual assets.

One person I know actively seeks out the criticism of those under him. "How am I doing?" "Is there anything you think I ought to know about *my* performance?" "Do you have any advice you could offer me?" Doing this would take more courage than most of us could muster. This guy actually thrives on it, and the more he does it, the stronger he seems to get.

Naturally, you have to use good judgment in what you ask of whom. Certain people do not seem to have the good sense to appreciate openness and will, therefore, only hurt you if you ask them their opinion. Most of us, however, tend to miss out on a great deal of personal and professional growth simply because we are afraid to hear honest evaluations of our own behavior. Moreover, the more you open yourself to criticism, the less it can wound you. As a general rule, the more we face the things we fear, the less we fear them. On the other hand, the fiery dragons of criticism become all the more ferocious when we run from them.

People who have the humility to listen, even when listening proves painful, tend to impress others as mature. They "come to honour" not only because they learn how to function better but also because others esteem them for their wisdom and stability.

When people take you to task, try to ask yourself if there is *anything* in what they say from which you might profit. Try to do this right when they are firing their salvos or taking their best shots. At very least, you can use the occasion as an opportunity to practice your poise. If you are too reactive to criticism, say to yourself: "I am not going to get sucked into defending myself by this guy or gal. What I am going to do is USE this moment to practice executive humility." Admittedly, these things are hard to do, but they are usually well worth the effort.

How do you generally respond to criticism?
Is there a way to respond to it more constructively?
Whose criticisms might you wisely seek out?

SELF-EVALUATION RATING: 1   2   3   4   5

NOTES AND REFLECTIONS:

Pride goes before destruction and haughtiness before a fall (Proverbs 16:18, TLB).

History books are full of stories of how pride, of one kind or another, led to the downfall of a ruler. Hitler, for example, sent thousands of young men to their unnecessary deaths simply because his pride would not allow him to see what would have been clear to any schoolchild: Germany had lost the war and The Thousand-Year Reich was over. Business, too, has its share of stories to illustrate that "pride goeth before a fall."

The news media gave much coverage to the criminal indictment of an ex-General Motors wonder boy who, during the 1980 recession, launched his own automotive company. While this man worked for GM, he had become exceedingly critical of the giant corporation. Apparently his independent business endeavor was as much a sincere protest as it was an entrepreneurial venture.

No doubt in part because of the depth of the recession, the car did not sell well, which placed its originator under considerable financial, and probably psychological, pressure. His response to poor sales was, according to his incredulous associates and employees, to *increase* production and, possibly, to become implicated in a multimillion-dollar cocaine sale. It seems as if the man's understandable pride in the car he created made it impossible for him simply to admit defeat and, perhaps, ultimately led to his downfall.

As human beings, pride is the one stance or position, above all others, that can be our undoing. It is pride that prompts us to defend ourselves and not to listen. It is pride that impels us to attack those who dare to imply that we are anything less than perfect. It is our pride that is injured, most of the time, when our feelings are hurt.

"God wants to cheat you. He says that he wants life's best, indeed his best for you, but you really cannot count on that. You only go around once, you know. Go for all the gusto you can. Don't wait for providence to make things fair in the end. Even the score now. *Take* what you know you should have." Sound familiar?

This is roughly what the serpent is reputed to have told Eve in the Garden of Eden. We all know the outcome. In response to the serpent's tauntings and allegations that God was actually a liar, Adam and Eve did what God had explicitly instructed them not to do. Thus they earned their exit visas from paradise.

All of us seem to carry around inside a hidden serpent. This fiend continually gets us right where it hurts, in the heart—in the pockets of our pride.

ME, ME, ME,
Worship ME;
I am more wonderful,
I am superior,
I am all that I could be,
Worship me, worship ME.

This is the sort of sick poem we recite unconsciously to ourselves. On the rocks of such stanzas, we stub our professional toes and fall on our personal faces.

Humankind's battle with pride goes back a long way. The ancient Greeks had a special word for pride, *hubris.* In the Greek tragedies, the protagonist was almost godlike. He had everything one could want. Unfortunately, he also routinely had this terrible, self-destructive pride. The Greek dramatists accurately perceived the lethality of pride and attempted to teach their contemporaries about its dangers. Their plays turn on the message, "Don't be like them, these men who lost everything through *hubris.*"

Be careful of defensive inflexibility, especially when it is combined with self-justification. Do not let pride ruin you. You are worth more to God and people than this!

Is there an area of your life in which you may be heading for trouble because of pride?

Is there something you should just own up to and let it go at that?

Can you allow yourself to admit that you are less than perfect, especially with respect to those things in which you take pride?

SELF-EVALUATION RATING: 1   2   3   4   5

NOTES AND REFLECTIONS:

GUIDELINE 27

Arrogance can inflame a city, but wisdom averts the people's anger (Proverbs 29:8, NEB); A fool is too arrogant to make amends; upright men know what reconciliation means (Proverbs 14:9, NEB).

The first of these two proverbs concerns arrogance by a person in authority, for example, by a boss. The second proverb has to do with ordinary relationships between people.

Arrogance in a ruler can be extremely provocative to those who are ruled. It can "inflame a whole city." Naturally, if the people who are ruled dare not speak out, the ruler may not know of their irritation and rage. It may stay hidden, underground, ready to surface at the first opportunity. This opportunity may be when the ruler is vulnerable, perhaps when the efficiency experts pass through or the management consultants come to do their climate surveys. If those who are governed see the ruler as arrogant enough, there may be open rebellion in any event, no matter what the cost to those who rebel.

Managers who keep themselves aloof from their subordinates may be taking a big chance, especially if these subordinates feel that they are being shunned because "they are not good enough, noble enough, smart enough, powerful enough, classy enough, educated enough," and so on and so forth. Holding yourself *above* others can be your downfall.

If you are the boss, then by definition you *are* above others in the organizational chart. They are, after all, your subordinates. But being in a certain position and, therefore, having to wield some power is not the same thing as communicating to others that you are superior to them as *people*.

One popular book on how to succeed in the corporate corridors recommends that a truly powerful executive *never* goes to the photocopying machine, even if he or she repaired it six months earlier. Photocopying is simply beneath the dignity of a star. It conveys weakness and the likelihood of a limited future career.

There may be something to this. As sad as it may be, and as tragic a commentary on human nature as it may seem, doing low-status things *may* hurt one's public image. Thus, doing them may injure one's chances for advancement. On the other hand, the leaders who have been most respected throughout history seem to be those who were not afraid to get their hands dirty with work or to fight alongside, if not in front of, their troops.

I recommend that you NEVER ask others to do what you yourself would not do. If you can photocopy, do it once in a while. If you can dial a phone, do that occasionally. If you can type, tune up your fingers now and then.

Obviously, the reason we sometimes have people working for us is so that they can do many of these routine tasks, and I am not suggesting that the corporation president suddenly begin wasting a lot of time—which is exactly what it would be—doing routine chores. I am suggesting, however, that you as boss communicate to your subordinates something like: "We're in this together. You have your job and I have mine, but we are both people. Nothing you do is, in principle, beneath me. Nothing I do is, in principle, above you."

Now, about arrogance as an obstacle to reconciliation: Many people, in their efforts to shore up their ailing self-images, adamantly refuse ever to say, "I'm sorry." They can neither forgive nor ask for others' forgiveness. Behind such people, almost always, are long trails of broken relationships. Most of these relationships could have been mended, healed, with just a little effort bathed in an ounce of repentance. Such people have enemies where they could have had friends. In business, this can be lethal.

Try to prevent yourself from developing the sort of arrogance that makes it impossible for one to say, "I was wrong." Place the restoration of relationships above pride.

Is there someone to whom you ought to communicate the message, "We're in this together, both important as people"?
With whom in your life do you have a strained or broken relationship?
Is there any sense in which arrogance is preventing reconciliation?

SELF-EVALUATION RATING: 1   2   3   4   5

NOTES AND REFLECTIONS:

One man wins success by his words; another gets his due reward by the work of his hands (Proverbs 12:14, NEB).

"Some people fix televisions. Some people plow fields. Some people manage pension plans. Some people drive taxis." There does not seem to be much profundity here. Clearly, different people make their livings in different ways. However, I believe that the proverb writer is hinting at something deeper, indeed, perhaps at several important ideas.

It is extremely important to find one's proper occupational niche. If one is best suited to fix computers, that is probably what one should do. If one is best suited to sell cars, *that* is probably what one should do. The computer wizard who sells Oldsmobiles and the car salesman who fixes IBM's are both badly situated. After years of experience consulting for a high-level career guidance center, I am thoroughly convinced that intelligent job selection is more than 50 percent of job success.

I am continually amazed at how many people know almost nothing about their true career aptitudes and interests. They know, for example, that they "like working with machines" or that they "are good with tasks that require lots of planning." But that is usually as far as it goes, if that far. Often they drift into jobs to which they are poorly suited and which promise to bring them very little in the way of personal satisfaction.

People who do not know their own interests and abilities are likely victims of the Peter Principle, which is that people tend to rise to the level of their incompetence. They continue to be promoted until they wind up in a job that they cannot do well. There they may remain for years: doing poorly what they should never have been doing in the first place.

I am currently working with someone who had always been brilliant doing a certain kind of job, so brilliant, in fact, that he got promoted a few years ago to a much higher-paying position doing an entirely *different* kind of job. Almost all of his energy is spent on sheer survival. The joy he used to take in his work has been replaced by dread. He worries about getting fired and senses that he is never going to be very effective at what he is doing.

Sometimes he marvels at others around him, for whom everything seems to come so easy. To him, they seem like naturals. The truth is that they would probably fall on their royal faces if they tried to do the job he *used* to do. I should add that, now that he is in the position he is, and is earning so much more money than he did before, it probably makes sense for him to continue to try to "survive." The emotional price of survival, however, is turning out to be considerable.

Because the rewards in our society are not distributed evenly, most of us live under tremendous pressure to move up. Many people are clawing their way to a top they will never see and, even if they did, one they would surely not enjoy. Not everyone is cut out to be a chief executive officer or board president. All of us have pockets of strength, regions of special ability and competence. The proverb writer is perhaps advising us to "play from our strengths" instead of our weaknesses. Perhaps he is also telling us that there are many noble ways to earn one's living. "Winning success by words" is not intrinsically superior to "winning success by the work of one's hands."

Evaluate your vocational assets and liabilities carefully—with ruthlessly candid humility. Do not let yourself be seduced by a few dollars into doing something for which you are not suited and which will never bring you fulfillment. Similarly, do not become a Peter Principle statistic. If you have to decline a promotion to remain successful, do it!

What are your best and worst job-related characteristics? (Remember: ruthlessly candid humility—truth above pride.)
Are you doing what you should be doing for a career?
Have you considered any kind of comprehensive career guidance?

SELF-EVALUATION RATING: 1   2   3   4   5

NOTES AND REFLECTIONS:

GETTING BY WITH WITH INTEGRITY

Kings take pleasure in honest lips; they value a man who speaks the truth (Proverbs 16:13, NIV).

Whom can the board member count on to tell the truth about the corporation's real financial position? To whom can the senior vice-president in charge of sales turn for realistic projections? Where is the chief executive officer who will tell the president when things are beginning to fall apart? Sometimes it is the "king" who is the last to know that the kingdom is crumbling.

Near the end of the book of Genesis, we read of how Joseph was sold into slavery by his brothers. Through a complicated series of events, Joseph eventually finds himself in Egypt, working in Pharaoh's court. Because of his integrity and competence, Joseph becomes a much-valued adviser to Pharaoh. In the end, because of his acquired power, Joseph helps the same brothers who years earlier tried to ruin him. Joseph's honesty with Pharaoh seems to have been a principal cause of his political ascendance.

People who wield great power, such as Egypt's imperial ruler, are forever being "rushed" by sycophants—those whose aim is to ingratiate themselves with the powerful. Like people with wealth, whom can the powerful trust? Who can be counted on to tell them the truth? Whose integrity is guaranteed? "Will someone, anyone, tell me the truth?" This is what I imagine many heads of state and many department heads and division managers muttering to themselves.

A friend of mine told me that, on the night someone he knew well was elected to high public office, he "heard from people he hadn't heard from in years." Perhaps these people were calling out of pure motives, possibly because the election reminded them of my friend. But can you be sure? Can my friend be sure that his callers were expressing genuine interest or congratulations? Or were they carefully crafting bits of verbal manipulation? For most of us to be terribly concerned with such questions would be a sign of psychopathology. For the powerful, however, these kinds of questions become the ever-present cloud hanging over almost every human encounter. Prominent people live lonely lives. They are sometimes surrounded by strangers only pretending to be friends.

Not only do the prominent have to worry about flattery; they also have to concern themselves with those who might betray their confidences. Anything they say can, and likely will, be used against them. As a White House budget director found out, you never know when your friend and confidant is going to write you up in a magazine article. Integrity or the lack of it—the issue seems to jump out at you from every public quarter. On whose word *can* you rely? Always there are temptations to betrayal. Always there are risks.

Just about all persons, corporation presidents included, want two things that are sometimes contradictory. On one hand, they want to hear the truth. On the other hand, they want to hear whatever will make them feel good at the moment. Thus, the person who presumes to speak with a powerful person is always potentially caught between the jaws of these sometimes competing demands. To be of real value to someone in power, you have to be willing to sacrifice favor for candor. This is no small achievement, given that powerful people can hurt you. Short of such extreme punishments as termination, there is—within the contemporary business world—banishment down the hall, denial of promotion, curtailment of perks, lagging salary increases, and so on.

To minimize the risk of being punished for your truthfulness, you must use consummate tact. Say things gently, perhaps even tentatively: "Perhaps ... maybe ... you may ... just a little ..." Recall our earlier proverb about a king's threat being like a lion's roar. Nonetheless, people of integrity are in extremely high demand with the powerful. If you can establish yourself as such a person, you will very likely reap rich rewards for your troubles.

Are you known to be trustable?
Do people see you as someone who will tell the truth, even at your own peril?
Do you temper your candor with wisdom? (Before you self-disclose, consider the likely impact of your candor.)

SELF-EVALUATION RATING: 1   2   3   4   5

NOTES AND REFLECTIONS:

GUIDELINE 30

He who rebukes a man will in the end gain more favor than he who has a flattering tongue (Proverbs 28:23, NIV).

Some research that was recently reported in a top psychology journal indicated that friends expect, indeed desire, confrontation from each other. While friendships are by nature supportive, they also serve as crucial forums for truth. "Only your best friends will tell you when . . ."

"John, let me say it straight . . ."

"Phyllis, look. No matter what you say, I have to tell you that . . ."

"Dan, you can react any way you want to, but I'm going to say what I have to say, which is that . . ."

John, Phyllis, and Dan are three of my closest friends. They would confront me just as quickly. Moreover, I would probably not expend this sort of energy, or take these kinds of interpersonal risks, for anyone other than a friend—unless, of course, it was my duty.

It *is* our duty. All social organizations have their unwritten norms for behavior, their codes of ethics. Part of our responsibility in the marketplace is to confront our associates, and even our customers, when it is in their best interests. Now, I do not deny that such confrontation is rarely done if there is even the slightest risk that it may backfire. Nevertheless, it is our duty!

The proverb goes even farther than this. It suggests that, in the end, the person who takes the risk of confronting will be more favored than the person who slides into the formless ooze of flattery. No one respects a person who can say only "sweet" things. If I have never heard you "say it straight," how can I trust you when you tell me how wonderful I am? But there is another reason why the person who "rebukes" wins more "favor."

It takes no genius to figure out that confrontation is inherently risky. After all, I could get angry with you, write you off, renounce you for your insensitivity, and so on, if you dare to confront me. If you confront me, then, it must mean either that you are too stupid to comprehend the risks involved, which is unlikely, that you are zapping me only because you want to get somebody, which is possible but not probable, or that you really CARE. Unless you *are* stupid or disturbed, you must be committed to me. If I sense this kind of commitment from you, I am very likely to make this kind of commitment to you . . . as soon as I get over my irritation, hurt, or what have you.

Just about anyone has the brains to realize that you have to be concerned to go out on a limb. To "take someone to task" (NEB, alt.) is to take the high road, the hard road, the road fraught with hazards and difficulties. It is ever so much easier just to say nothing and "let everything pass." Having the courage and fortitude to confront another person in a loving manner, and with a loving intent, is very much evidence of virtue. Note that this is not to advocate chewing out people or ripping them to emotional shreds. It *is* to advocate, in the words of a best-selling book, "caring enough to confront."

A well-known football coach once said that the reason he drove his team so hard was that, by his doing so, his players would feel good about themselves regardless of how the season turned out. "If I'm soft on them, they'll always wonder if we could have won. If I pull everything out of them that they can give, there will be no wondering. We'll all know we did our best."

Our friends, associates, and subordinates want to know that they did their best. At very least, they want to know that they had the means at their disposal to do their best, regardless of whether they chose to do it. Sometimes what they need, only we have: truth.

Take the risk of telling the truth, only do it graciously. Test the proverb writer's thesis that, in the long run, straight talk will win you more appreciation than flattery.

To what extent do you flatter others?
Are there people you should confront and, if so, how can you do this most
  effectively? (As a general principle, use minimum necessary force.)

SELF-EVALUATION RATING: 1   2   3   4   5

NOTES AND REFLECTIONS:

GUIDELINE 31

A little, gained honestly, is better than great wealth gotten by dishonest means (Proverbs 16:8, TLB); The upright man is secure in his own honesty (Proverbs 14:32b, NEB).

A popular myth, especially among those who are bitter about not having more money, is that money has nothing to do with happiness. This is plainly false. There is overwhelming evidence to suggest that money and happiness *are* positively correlated. Having money may not, strictly speaking, cause happiness, but it can help, provided that one's attitude toward money is wholesome and not pathological.

Money cannot *guarantee* happiness or fulfillment. This is obvious if you stop to think about it for a moment. The richest person in the world, when faced by personal tragedy, hurts every bit as much as the poorest person in similar straits. So, money may be a good thing, but it is not totally satisfying, which is why the Bible warns us not to make money our god.

Money can be a tool for peace. It can give you, for example, a certain freedom from economic worry. To be able to pay all your bills without hesitation is a comforting reality, while to worry about how you're going to make ends meet this week is not.

Treachery, however, tends to ruin peace. As a result, if you acquire money in order to have peace, through treacherous means—which are almost certain to destroy peace—you pull yourself in opposite directions. Unless you are a total psychopath—someone without a conscience—you will not feel contented if you have come by your wealth dishonestly. Your guilt will get you. For a time you may be able to forget the nature of what you have done, but sooner or later it will probably come back to haunt you.

Even if you can avoid being haunted by guilt, the fruits of your treachery may come back to poison your life. You may have to pay back corrupt favors. You may have to withstand the hatred or scorn of those you wronged. You may even have to go to jail. The odds of achieving satisfaction by means of corruptly acquired wealth seem slim indeed.

As the second proverb suggests, honesty carries with it a certain inner security, a tranquillity of the soul. There is something tremendously reassuring about *knowing* that every penny you have has been earned honestly. Two thousand dollars earned with integrity may provide far more satisfaction than twenty thousand dollars acquired dishonestly. To some extent, the value of money is determined by the value *you* place on it. Money's worth is not established simply by the goods and services it will command. Part of the equation is how much you want these goods and services and how you feel about your own financial resources and the ways by which you have come into them.

Work hard. Save, little by little, and invest wisely. Eventually, if it is God's will, you will prosper and get to enjoy some of the truly wonderful things that money can buy, including freedom from financial worry. Do not let yourself fall into the habit of getting your money in dishonest ways or you will be potentially throwing away the very thing you are trying to acquire: satisfaction. Peace of mind is essential to satisfaction.

To what extent, if any, are your ways of acquiring money compromised? How could you fully achieve the security that comes from honesty?

SELF-EVALUATION RATING: 1   2   3   4   5

NOTES AND REFLECTIONS:

GUIDELINE 32

Charm is deceptive, and beauty is fleeting; but a woman who fears the LORD is to be praised. Give her the reward she has earned, and let her works bring her praise at the city gate (Proverbs 31:30–31, NIV).

The author is saying, in essence, that character and spirituality are, ultimately, far more important and worthwhile than smooth skin, lean curves, or low cellulite (or, turning things around, tanned and muscular Adonis bodies). Physical characteristics, however enjoyable, fade. No one with red blood denies the pleasurable aspects of physical beauty, which is exactly why this proverb was written. It is intended to get us to see the reality behind appearances.

Despite the effects of the women's movement, there still exist substantial inequalities between men and women. Men, in general, are more powerful. Many women live in a kind of economic servitude to abusive spouses, and for complex reasons, most women are more marriageable the younger they are. Men, on the other hand, generally do not peak out until perhaps their late forties or early fifties. Consequently, while a woman's marriageability declines with age, a man's increases.

Over time, this places the man in an ever more favorable relative position with respect to the cold, hard marketplace. I have provided psychological services to many women who had been left by husbands who took up with younger women. The proverb writer, over two thousand years ago, was sensitive to this inequity. He is telling men that they have no right to trade in their wives for newer models! To do this is to cheat the woman out of what is due her: praise, honor, respect, and recognition.

When you marry, you are making what is supposed to be a permanent commitment. This, at least, is what the words in marriage vows typically say. Although, as ethicist Lewis Smedes points out, marriage is better thought of as a covenant ("I will be something to you and you will be something to me") than a service agreement ("I'll do these things for you if you'll do these things for me"), the idea of a contract is sufficiently robust to remind us of what marriage is intended to be—binding.

I am not attempting to induce guilt into people who have been divorced, nor am I trying to make men feel bad who might have done some of the things we are considering. I am, however, highlighting the penetrating truth of "charm is a delusion and beauty fleeting" (NEB). Today we might put it this way: charm can be *extremely* deceptive; it is capable of enchanting one, to the point that one can come to believe what is patently bizarre, namely, that charm can satisfy the soul. A delusion *is* a firmly held bizarre belief.

Some straight talk to my fellowmen: You may find yourself from time to ime taken, perhaps enamoured, with someone at the office or elsewhere. f so, don't be too hard on yourself. You are human. If you have ideas of acting on your infatuations, FORGET IT. I am writing not as a moralist but as a psychologist who has seen much heartache and destruction come to both pack-the-suitcase-and-split men and left-on-the-doorstep women.

Straight talk to women: Almost any man who would become involved with you while you are married is a terrible risk. If he truly wants to break up your family on the thesis that the two of you will live happily ever after, WATCH OUT. Such a man will, if he is trading in one wife now, possibly trade in another one later! Do NOT run off with the power magnate, no matter what he promises you.

All of this, of course, is also true in reverse. Men can also be deceptively charming. And, the businesswoman who breaks up a man's marriage today may trade *him* in farther down the line.

Perhaps I am being too blunt. It's just that I've witnessed all that pain.

Do you sufficiently honor those you should?
If and when you are tempted, do you count the costs of acting on your temptations? (These costs may cause the erosion of your integrity as well as your bank account.)

SELF-EVALUATION RATING: 1   2   3   4   5

NOTES AND REFLECTIONS:

A good man leaves an inheritance to his descendants (Proverbs 13:22, NEB).

Life insurance that you take out on yourself is an investment whose "profits" you will, by definition, never live to enjoy. Purchasing such insurance, unless in the interests of gaining immediate economic or social advantage, is perhaps as close to pure altruism as many people ever come.

The impossibility of being the beneficiary of your own life insurance policy is perhaps why so many people do not buy one. While the reluctance of some may stem from a need to deny the inevitability of their own death, or even the conviction that they can best protect their loved ones by investing in something other than insurance, some people just do not want to part with the premiums.

Any form of wealth that we set aside for the express purpose of bequeathing it to others represents something that we are giving away. The proverb writer is suggesting that this kind of giving is characteristic of a "good" person. Buying life insurance is, of course, only one way of building an estate.

Society sometimes rewards us for doing good things. For example, on the assumption that saving money is desirable for everyone, we are permitted to deduct modest amounts of earned interest in our tax calculations. Similarly, there are economic advantages connected with building up various kinds of inheritances, for example, trusts for one's children. Let us set such immediate advantages aside, however, to consider some of the less obvious benefits of knowing that one will be "leaving an inheritance to one's descendants."

First, most of us have at least some ambivalence about making money. Although there is nothing wrong with money itself, the inordinate *love* of money, relative to other potential objects of our love (e.g., God and people), can cause us problems. Because we correctly sense that the quest for money can become a spiritual and emotional disease, some of us unconsciously (but nonetheless determinedly) avoid acquiring much of it. Nothing cures such self-sabotage like knowing that you want money for good reasons. Most people would agree that trying to amass money for the future benefit of loved ones is definitely a good reason! Imagine how unconflicted you would be about making money if you suddenly needed lots of it to save the life of a child.

Second, putting together some kind of inheritance for your dependents is a very direct expression of love. While many cynical people would debate this, love has a way of coming back to you. The giver *is* sometimes blessed as much, if not more, than the receiver. It seems to be built into the cosmos that when you do things for others, YOU prosper. Most people have had the experience of profiting substantially from something that they did for others, without any view toward personal benefit.

Third, and most important of all, there is simply an inner peace in knowing that you are doing the right things. Goodness *is* its own reward, certainly psychologically. You cannot be happy for long without peace.

While the question of just how much money you should leave to others is a highly personal one, there are good reasons for setting aside something for this purpose. I recommend that you do it as part of an overall program of integrity. Such integrity helps instead of hinders successful living.

Do you work entirely for yourself, or do your goals include enhancing the welfare of others?

Are you systematically accumulating "an inheritance to leave to your descendants"? (Life insurance may or may not be a prudent investment, depending on one's age and assets.)

SELF-EVALUATION RATING: 1   2   3   4   5

NOTES AND REFLECTIONS:

MATURITY AND JUDGMENT

To be patient shows intelligence; to overlook faults is a man's glory (Proverbs 19:11, NEB); Patience heals discords (Proverbs 15:18b, NEB); The man in a hurry misses the way (Proverbs 19:2b, NEB).

When you live in the kind of fast-paced world that we live in, it is not easy to be patient. If efficiency is not our god, it is certainly among our highest values. In just about every one of our endeavors, most particularly in business, the idea is to get there first. Rush, run, race! This insane emphasis on speed tends to work against good judgment. It also tends to injure relationships. All three of these proverbs highlight an important aspect of patience.

Patience, to begin with, reflects a certain kind of social intelligence. Think of those persons in your life who, even though they may not have to be, are patient with you. Do they not strike you as wise and intelligent? The "glory" of patience comes from seeing the bigger picture, from *not* being so petty that one gets hung up on the trivial. A patient person can move quickly, even rush intensely when necessary. The issue is how tolerant we are of others and of uncertainty.

Not only does patience help you get along well in the world, but it also helps you help others to get along well. Patience is reflected in an ability to *hear* their concerns. This, in turn, allows you to bring healing, which in business can make the difference between great success and terrible failure. If you have a talent for soothing hurt feelings, you carry with you the potential to salvage nearly lost accounts, almost breached contracts, and so on. Moreover, by not rushing in with superficial solutions or, worse, to express your own grievances, you give other people the time and mental space they need to work out their problems, resolve their tensions, and settle their disagreements. As a rule, the farther people get away from an upsetting event, and the more time that passes, the more they seem to be able to come to terms with what, at first, may have been totally unacceptable to them.

Finally, patience allows you to see the way instead of missing it! How many times have you searched frantically for something but, because you were in such a hurry, you did not see it when it was right in front of you? Brilliance is sometimes the capacity to see the obvious. Yet nothing can be obvious to you if you do not take the time to look. Let me show you how "obvious" something can be—once someone points it out to you.

Question: What is it about a wheel that makes it such a clever invention or, to state the question differently, What makes a wheel a wheel? (A wheel is not just something round. Egyptians used logs on which to roll huge stones, but these logs were not wheels. A wheel has a *fixed* axle, i.e., a cylinder that rotates about a shaft that is stably attached to a vehicle of some sort. Some civilizations used wheels to make toys, apparently without thinking to use them to do work.)

Question: What was the primary military value of the Great Wall of China, other than its function as a series of lookout posts that could quickly relay communications? (Warriors could use ladders to climb over the thirty-foot wall; they could not get their horses over it. Thus the Hun invaders were turned away from China.)

Some of us are, by nature, more patient than others. Certain people move very quickly while others move very slowly. Some are high-strung while others are easygoing. Such traits are partly due to how our bodies are constructed, but they also relate to how we are put together *psychologically* and, indeed, to how we have trained ourselves. Within limits, you CAN alter your own "speeds." If you are impulsive, practice looking before you leap. If you are intolerant, practice toleration. If you are high-strung, practice being mellow. Change may not come easily, but with dedicated effort it *will* come.

Learning more patience will probably increase your social intelligence, your ability to help others, and your capacity to notice what others tend to miss because *they* are in such a hurry. Gaining control of your psychological speedometer will make you more likely to move at the right speed in whatever situation you find yourself.

In which particular situations is it most difficult for you to be patient?
With which people are you the most impatient?
How might you develop more patience? (Suggestion: Spend some time every day imagining situations in which you tend to act impatiently, only visualize yourself being very calm, slow, circumspect.)

SELF-EVALUATION RATING: 1   2   3   4   5

NOTES AND REFLECTIONS:

GUIDELINE 35

It is a trap for a man to dedicate something rashly and only later to consider his vows (Proverbs 20:25, NIV).

Another psychologist once came to visit me and, while in my office, noticed that I had several copies of a book he very much wanted. The book was relatively expensive and I had purposely acquired multiple copies so that, when it went out of print, as eventually nearly all books do, I would be able to lend them to my students.

"Why don't you lend me one of these and I'll give you one back when it comes from the publisher?"

"Here," I replied, "just take one. Keep it. I have several."

I should have said, "No, I'd prefer to hold on to all of these," or even, "Okay, I'll lend you one if you promise to replace it." What I did, in fact, was a classic example of what psychoanalysts call reaction formation (substituting in consciousness the antithesis of what one thinks unconsciously, e.g., little boys and girls "hating" each other as soon as they begin to feel the stirrings of attraction to members of the other sex). I said the opposite of what I really felt, only it happened so quickly that I scarcely had time to think about my own words. Later I grieved over the loss of the treasured volume!

The problem with what I did was that it was not from the heart. I was not a "cheerful giver." I did not have the inner love to follow through on my own offer.

Not all rashly given gifts or hastily made commitments are reaction formations however. Sometimes we genuinely intend to give the gift or make the promise, only we do not stop to count the cost. Later, when we realize the expense involved, we have second thoughts and occasionally deep regret. "What did I get myself into?" We "danced" to the joy of our own generosity and now it is time to pay the piper.

The proverb is warning against poorly thought out commitments. "Think through what you do before you do it. Don't offer, promise, or give what you do not want to, or what you will later resent."

Naturally, there are exceptions. If you find someone draped in blood lying in the gutter, there is no merit in refusing to help, simply because you might later "resent" it. Still, in the ordinary course of things, it is not good to offer what you cannot deliver willingly. All behaviors have consequences. The consequences of good behaviors sometimes have to be thought through just as much as the potential consequences of bad ones.

Resentment is an especially lethal emotion. It destroys friendships. It probably also causes heart attacks. Resentment tends to eat you up from the inside, thus seriously hindering your effectiveness. In addition, other people can usually tell when you resent them or your obligations to them, which is particularly insidious when *you* established these obligations through your own grand words.

Commit your time, energy, and belongings *only* after you engage in enough reflection to ensure that you will not later regret having made these commitments. Many of us tend often to get in our own way. We become our own worst obstacles, sometimes by placing unnecessary constraints on ourselves. Carefully avoid creating "traps" for yourself by making impulsive commitments.

Do you tend to commit too quickly?
Are there particular areas (e.g., time) where you are most vulnerable?
Are there particular people to whom you too readily make commitments?

SELF-EVALUATION RATING: 1   2   3   4   5

NOTES AND REFLECTIONS:

GUIDELINE 36

A shrewd man sees trouble coming and lies low; the simple walk into it and pay the penalty (Proverbs 22:3, NEB).

A lemming is a small rodent that resembles a mouse. For complex reasons that relate to local overpopulation in their species, every three or four years hoards of European lemmings begin frantically to search for new territory. In their single-minded search, they ignore all obstacles. The lemmings inadvertently race toward high precipices, bound over them, and plunge to their deaths. This proverb warns us not to follow in the footsteps of the lemmings.

All of us have blind spots, areas of our lives in which we are vulnerable simply because we are insufficiently perceptive. Some people are easy marks for confidence artists. Others continually lose at corporate "hot potato," such that they get caught with the blame for mistakes and negligences not their own. Some people do not seem to notice when aggressions escalate and, as a result, become embroiled in senseless battles. Some habitually get involved with people who wrap them up in emotional flypaper, immensely complicating their lives with ridiculous hassles and misunderstandings. Some are "too good" for their own good; they help people who either do not want help or who actually repay kindness with malice.

As a psychotherapist I have had to learn to be prudent in how I expend my energies. Over the years it has become relatively easy to spot certain kinds of potential trouble and, thus, to avoid it. For example, I have learned to sense when someone is likely to be financially unreliable (translation: not pay me for my hard work), excessively demanding (translation: lots of unnecessary phone calls, paper work, etc.), or chronically dissatisfied (translation: no matter what I do, the person will complain). Learning to do this was not easy, and I am getting better at it all the time. To the degree that I improve my vision, things go ever so much more smoothly for me!

In your profession, you may have to watch out for different kinds of things. For example, you may have to be very careful in what you say to some people, lest they betray your confidences, or you may need to be ever on the alert for the possibility of legal trouble. Every occupation has its special hazards. You can ignore them only at great peril. Relatedly, every person has particular vulnerabilities, whether the tendency to trust too much or too little, to risk too much or too little, and so on. For example, you may tend to hire people who are occupational time bombs or to ask the wrong people for help and advice.

Spending a few minutes each day with a pad and pencil will assist you to spot those things which might cause you trouble. Routinely evaluate the pros and cons of your alternatives, as well as the strong and weak points of the individuals with whom you associate, especially those on whom you have to rely. What potential troubles could ensue from the actions you contemplate taking? What do you have to watch out for with particular people? Such evaluations may seem cold and calculating. However, those people who have nothing to hide do not worry excessively about audits. As far as thorough "interpersonal audits," your friends won't mind 'em, and your enemies won't survive 'em!

You have to be willing to FACE reality to learn from it. If you truly want to do better in the future, find out where you have done worse in the past. Deliberately look for your own mistakes. I don't know about you, but I have made a lot of them. Keep in mind that old adage about how people who know nothing about history are doomed to repeat it. What is true of global history is perhaps even more applicable to individual history. Be astute in finding out which of life's punches most often nail you. When do you forget to duck?

Looking back over your entire life, what sorts of dangers did you fail to see coming?

To what extent do you have a "lemming instinct," such that your single-mindedness leads you over the precipice?

What kinds of things might you need to pay special attention to so that you do not miss seeing them?

SELF-EVALUATION RATING: 1   2   3   4   5

NOTES AND REFLECTIONS:

GUIDELINE 37

Develop your business first before building your house (Proverbs 24:27, TLB).

This proverb is about fundamental economic priorities. While it certainly concerns money, by implication it also has to do with the wider spheres of time and energy. The writer is advising us to establish intelligent priorities and to stick to them. "First, solidly establish your source of income. Then, and only then, turn your attention to other things which, while fine in themselves, will only distract you from what ought to be your primary aim: solvency. Don't divert your energies into worrying about the house you live in (unless this relates to your earnings), where you're going to hang your favorite pictures, or whether the hedge is to be two or three feet high. Maintain your focus, your concentration, on *developing* your business."

The proverb is not exhorting us to neglect our loved ones or to become "work compulsives" who use their careers to run away from intimacy with people. It is perhaps saying: "Don't retreat from the hard business of making a living, into a fantasy world. Go out and cut it! Make your way. Do not be lazy or timid. Try to ensure the well-being of yourself and your family. Rather than lulling yourself to sleep by becoming soft or confused about your priorities, decide what you want and go after it."

A few weeks ago I realized that, as a family, we had too much personal property in proportion to our real property. In other words, our house is too small to hold all the stuff we own. This, I think, reflects some sloppy priority-setting, or perhaps just a plain lack of proper priority-setting! It is not that we own anything that is especially expensive, only that we own a lot of things that are not especially inexpensive. While we enjoy what we have—especially all those books!—I think we would have been wiser to save some of the money that we simply spent on things.

Few of us, of course, think and act with the rational efficiency of robots. We do much of what we do for emotionally toned reasons, some good, some bad, some wise, and some stupid. Because we are *human* beings and not collections of silicone chips, our motivations and thus our satisfactions can be exceedingly complex. We want this because it is the right shade of blue, and not that because it is the wrong shade of green. You cannot reduce your life to a software package or to a double-entry ledger without seriously tarnishing its existential luster.

Nevertheless, God gave us minds with which to *think*. Refusing to set down explicit priorities is to sentence yourself to live out implicit ones. It is a little like all that business about how *not* to make a decision is, in fact, to make a decision. This proverb contains guidance about how to make decisions: usually according to what will, in the long run, best establish the economic security of yourself and your family. Such advice does tend to generate some internal tension.

As a writer, for example, I do not like it because I very much want to write a novel. There is only one problem. Just about all first novels lose money, that is, assuming you can even get somebody to publish them! So, as much as I would prefer some days to stay home and work on my partially finished novel, I trundle off to another consulting job. Lord permitting, I *will* complete my novel, but wisdom dictates that I do so only when I can afford the immediate curtailment of income.

Make sure you have a sensible plan for "developing your business," and distribute your resources according to it. Taking into consideration the fact that there is never enough time to do everything one would like, keep your personal and professional life in proper balance. There are always those trade-offs and sacrifices. Life demands that we make choices. Love yourself enough—as God loves you—to make them wisely.

What do you want to accomplish in business this year, and in the years ahead?

Are your energies distributed to maximize the probability that you will achieve your goals?

Are you making the right sacrifices while refusing to make the wrong ones?

SELF-EVALUATION RATING: 1   2   3   4   5

NOTES AND REFLECTIONS:

A man who deceives another and then says, "It was only a joke," is like a madman shooting at random his deadly darts and arrows (Proverbs 26:19, 18, NEB).

Suppose you were walking along a city street, amid high-rise buildings and congested thoroughfares, and someone wearing a surveyor's hat asked you to hold one end of a blue string. "It will only take a few minutes," he assures you. "My assistant is home sick today, and I badly need someone to help me with this measurement by holding this line tight." Or, suppose you were driving through the same crowded city during the middle of a business day and rounded a busy corner, only to feel your front right wheel roll into a ditch.

Imagine, further, that after you had faithfully held the blue string for over fifteen minutes, your irritation ever mounting, you walked around the corner and found another bewildered pedestrian holding on to the other end. Imagine also that, upon getting out of your car and determining that your front axle had cracked under the impact of the fall, all the while listening to the abuses of other drivers whose way you had blocked, you discovered that the road had been dug up as a practical joke.

These are actual situations. At least once, a busy New York street was dug up by impostors, and the "string sting" is, unfortunately, exercised frequently on people who, the next time they are asked to help, do so with rather more reluctance.

Some people have what I can only take to be a perverse pleasure in playing "jokes" on others. Clinically, most practical jokers are merely acting out their hostilities, or bolstering their senses of importance by victimizing others. The sickest part of the whole thing is when they say: "I was only kidding. Why are you getting so upset? It was just a joke." Most people who routinely play practical jokes on others want to be nasty without having to pay the price for their hostility. They expect to get away with imposing all kinds of discomforts on others under the guise of good-hearted humor. As psychoanalysts point out, however, there are no jokes. Beneath just about every joke is some kind of serious statement or intention.

Does this mean that we ought to go around with sour faces, unable to appreciate what is funny or to laugh at the genuinely absurd? Not at all. Wholesome humor does relieve tension and, at times, makes life more bearable.

It *does* mean that, if you are going to be hostile, you ought at least to admit to yourself, and to others, the nature of what you are doing. Mature people do not hide behind apologies or appeals to humor. If they get caught in some act of aggression or even in a deception, they are not so naive as to try to explain it away with a ridiculous claim like, "I was only fooling." Such statements are primitive, if not pathetic, forms of what psychologists call "undoing." Undoing is the defense of trying magically to turn back the clock. It is an attempt to wriggle out of having to face the consequences of what we have done.

The proverb is making the strong statement that deceptions, especially when people try to cover them over with foolish excuses, can be deadly. More than one person has died because another person who was the brunt of a "joke" turned out not to have much of a sense of humor. Similarly, more than one up-and-coming business person has been shunted off to Occupational Never-Never Land, or even fired, because of an overdeveloped, if not marginally psychotic (psychosis is a form of mental disorder in which one cannot distinguish fantasy from reality), sense of humor.

Be careful about making jokes, especially since they tend to give away some of our baser impulses and instincts. Let others call to mind your maturity and good judgment long before they remember your funnies or your witticisms.

Are you at all prone to making hostile comments, or doing aggressive
    things, and then excusing them as jokes?
Are there people around you who are dangerous, and therefore ought to
    be avoided, because they like to victimize others with their "jokes"?

SELF-EVALUATION RATING: 1   2   3   4   5

NOTES AND REFLECTIONS:

GUIDELINE 39

Argue your own case with your neighbor, but do not reveal another man's secret, or he will reproach you when he hears of it and your indiscretion will then be beyond recall (Proverbs 25:9–10, NEB).

When I arrived in California, I was horrified by a psychotherapist who readily boasted about the movie stars he "had in therapy." Perhaps the stars did not mind. From time to time, it has been fashionable to have an analyst. Still, I always had the impression that this therapist was a little too quick to use the people he was no doubt sincerely trying to help in order to enhance his own reputation. Stars, after all, are people too. Like the rest of us, they hurt, they bleed, and they need privacy. Let me add that most therapists are *extremely* careful about honoring confidences. They would not betray a client if their fingernails were pulled out!

Even if you are not a psychotherapist, when someone gives you personal information, an implied contract is established. Just by listening, you are usually conveying the impression that you will treat what you hear as sensitive material. This implies, in turn, that you will not opportunistically use it for your own advantage.

Let us assume, for the sake of illustration, that you get into a minor argument with one of your neighbors, say, because he tends to accumulate unsightly piles of used car parts on his front lawn. He is clearly downgrading the neighborhood. When you ask him tactfully to remove some of the debris, he launches into a defensive speech. Your anxiety mounts and you become a little agitated. Finally, in exasperation, you say: "Look, Stan. I'm not the only one on the block who is concerned about all this junk. Harry was saying the same thing just the other day." Oops!

Harry entrusted you with his private opinion, with which you have now gone "public." Perhaps Stan will forget what you said. On the other hand, he may tell Harry what you said *he* said. This could result in an awful mess, including the ruination of long-standing friendships, all because of a few careless words. The courses of wars have been influenced by even fewer words.

In the business world, information takes on almost as high a value as it does in war. Corporations pay huge sums of money for certain kinds of information, ranging from the results of industrial espionage to financial advisory services. Companies hire consultants. Wall Street buffs read *The Wall Street Journal.* IBM annually makes millions by providing businesses with the means by which to store and digest information. The intelligence market is, indeed, big business.

It is sometimes tempting to use what one knows to get ahead, even if this means violating someone else in the process. Good "corporate players," in fact, are often adroit at manipulating out of others confidential utterances whose value, in kind, they never intend to repay. Fortunately, such information manipulators often become known for what they are, to the advantage of everyone else.

Watch what you say. You could easily make an inveterate enemy out of someone whose confidence you violate. Alliances, if they are to be more than fleeting marriages of convenience, have to be built solidly on trust. You and the other person have to *know* that there will be no leaks, no down-the-river sales.

Are you sufficiently careful about what you say, especially when the information could prove damaging to others?

Are you known as a person who respects confidences?

Are there certain people toward whom you *should* be on guard, because of their slick abilities to get others to talk too much?

SELF-EVALUATION RATING: 1   2   3   4   5

NOTES AND REFLECTIONS:

GUIDELINE 40

Don't visit your neighbor too often, or you will outwear your welcome (Proverbs 25:17, TLB).

Let us first consider the other side of the argument. Does familiarity ever breed not contempt but fondness?

A good deal of research evidence now suggests that, in general, the more frequently people have contact, the more they like each other. Simple proximity—closeness—does seem to increase attraction and affection. Most of us, for example, occasionally long to return to the place where we were raised. We miss it as well as the people with whom we grew up.

It is interesting that some people stubbornly cling to certain manners of speech, for instance, the use of double negatives or slang words, not only through force of habit but because such utterances *psychologically* signify to them what, and whom, they long ago came to love. We have strong preferences for the familiar.

Like most generalizations, however, the "contact breeds liking" principle has to be qualified. First, if people are obnoxious, being around them more often is not going to endear them to us. If anything, it will only make us like them less.

Second, when proximity is combined with intense competition, people come not to love but to hate each other. Concentration camps provide evidence for this, but more immediate proof comes from affluent suburbs inhabited by junior executives from the same company. Mutual character assassination is common in such socially competitive areas.

Third, like animals only more so, human beings have a definite love for novelty (which is sometimes stronger than their love of the familiar). This is why Christmas toys become old so fast, to the emotional and economic dismay of the loving parents who bought them. Our quest for the novel is also the mainstay for the mass entertainment industries. While shows, movies, and so on, do sometimes provide us with aesthetically pleasing and educationally beneficial experiences, we probably value them most for their capacities to provide us with ever-new forms of stimulation.

Finally, people value their solitude. If God wanted us not to have any privacy, he would have endowed us with mental telepathy. I am sure that he did not elect to do so, in this life at least, because we could not take the strain! As John Steinbeck wisely put it, we need to be together but we also need to be alone. Consider how much in vogue it is these days to speak of "having one's own space."

The author of this proverb is perhaps warning us against symbiosis. A symbiotic relationship is one in which two living things provide necessary services to each other. The entire plant and animal kingdoms are, at large, symbiotic when it comes to oxygen and carbon dioxide. Plants make oxygen and use carbon dioxide, while animals make carbon dioxide and use oxygen.

The problem with symbiotic relationships between human beings is that such arrangements tend to deprive the participants of their respective identities and freedoms. People ordinarily resent such deprivation, although often they are not conscious of exactly what it is that they resent. Often, they just feel irritable or restless.

In a business environment, people are easily frightened by what they, rightly or wrongly, perceive as excessive dependence. Form alliances. Enjoy regular associations. Make friends. Only be careful that you do not crowd others too much, since what you may intend as warmth and camaraderie, they may experience as suffocation. Absence does sometimes "make the heart grow fonder."

Are you maintaining the right psychological distances with others, neither too close nor too far away?
Is there someone at this moment to whom you ought to grant more "psychological space," whether a superior, a subordinate, or a peer?

SELF-EVALUATION RATING: 1   2   3   4   5

NOTES AND REFLECTIONS:

GUIDELINE 41

A fool shows his ill humour at once; a clever man slighted conceals his feelings. An honest speaker comes out with the truth, but the false witness is full of deceit. Gossip can be sharp as a sword, but the tongue of the wise heals (Proverbs 12:16–18, NEB).

Although these proverbs concern the proper use of the tongue, a subject we explored earlier, I elected to discuss them here because they seem so central to what we ordinarily mean by *maturity.* I feel the need to emphasize the close connection between public speech and private wisdom.

First, an immature person reacts immediately when he or she is irritated. A mature person, on the other hand, "stays cool" (TLB).

Second, an honest and by implication a mature speaker says what is true, while a dishonest one is "full of deceit." These statements were probably written down to underscore the relationship between what we do and our reputations, and perhaps also between our hearts and our lips. People who routinely speak the truth are known for their honesty. For them, truth is a way of life.

Third, we can cut others with gossip, which always carries with it the potential to injure. Or we can use our words to heal.

These proverbs exhort us to anticipate the effects of what we say. People are social beings as well as spiritual, psychological, political, economic, and physiological ones. All of us are susceptible to how others talk to, and about, us. Their words can soothe or inflame us, comfort or distress us, build up our reputations or tear them down.

Spontaneity, as much as its value is touted these days, is not always a virtue. Too much spontaneity smacks of irresponsibility and plunges society into chaos. Violent criminals are excellent examples of overdeveloped spontaneity. Having never learned to limit how much they act on their impulses, they simply do what they feel like doing, when they feel like doing it. Spontaneity, to be healthy, has to be balanced by control.

Take things easy when it comes to expressing displeasure or irritation. You can always do *that.* Once you lash out, however, it is hard to undo the effects of your actions. If someone angers you or hurts your feelings, let it ride for a while. Later, if you wish, you can launch into combat, but if you unthinkingly blurt out your reactions, things can quickly get out of hand and beyond your ability to regulate. *Timing* is all-important. There is a time to confront, and a time to hold off and plan exactly what you want to say.

These three sayings deal with the effects of public communication. How we make others look in public is a very important determinant of how they feel about us. It is just not smart to put others into a position where they feel that they must attack in order to preserve their honor. "Blasting them" with your words, lying about them "on the stand" (one translation: to the boss), or gossiping about their frailties and indiscretions is certain to kindle their ire.

All of this gets even more complicated when you consider the fact that some people *feel* slighted when, in fact, no one has slighted them. While you cannot make yourself responsible for anyone else's "paranoid sensitivity," people with good social intelligence take into account the other person's "P.S. Factor" before acting.

Practice "keeping cool," speaking only the truth, and resisting the temptation to be drawn into gossip. People will usually give you, or put you in charge of, their resources *only* if they trust you. They decide whether to trust you largely on the basis of your verbal behavior.

Do you pause sufficiently before showing your "ill humour"?
Are you known for your mature honesty, so that others find themselves automatically trusting what you say?
Do you use your words to heal?

SELF-EVALUATION RATING: 1   2   3   4   5

NOTES AND REFLECTIONS:

AVOIDING SELF-DESTRUCTION

The accomplice of a thief is his own enemy (Proverbs 29:24, NIV); He who sends a fool on an errand cuts his own leg off and displays the stump (Proverbs 26:6, NEB); Don't associate with evil men (Proverbs 23:6, TLB).

We have all heard that there is supposed to be "honor among thieves." Do not believe it! People who steal from the customer or the company are just as likely to steal from you. To depend on the honor of a thief is to beg to be robbed.

A friend of mine put everything he had into developing a business with another person who, ultimately, turned out to be unsavory. My friend's business associate was anything but an overt thief, but when it came time to lock in the ownership of the company, the associate got greedy. As far as I know, my friend has yet to realize a dime for all his hard work.

As this illustration shows, accurate character assessment can be pivotal to success. All thieves are *not* cat burglars who conveniently identify themselves by their black tights, or convicted embezzlers with stripes across their chests. Some are truly nice people who have only one or two episodes of larceny during their entire lives. Unfortunately, it only takes one such episode to ruin you, if you are its victim. So the first lesson in this quick course in how to avoid self-ruin is to evaluate carefully the other person's R.O.T. ("rip off tendency"). Among the best ways to do yourself in is to form a partnership, formal or otherwise, with someone whose R.O.T. is high.

Another way to hurt yourself is to choose a "fool" as your agent. Anyone who acts on your behalf with your permission is your agent, whether as assistant, messenger, accountant, attorney, seller, or buyer. Fools, almost by definition, muck things up. When a fool is acting as your agent, *you* are the person responsible for whatever mess ensues. Other people, noting the kind of representative you select, tend to conclude that it takes one to pick one. Protect yourself! Do NOT give the power to represent you to *anyone* who will not represent you well. Picking the right agent for the right job is far more important than selecting the right clothes to wear, and think of all the attention we give to that. If you choose your agents unwisely, you are, in the stark words of the proverb writer, "cutting off your own leg and displaying the stump."

The third proverb has been translated in several ways. "Do not go to dinner with a miser" (NEB) is one alternative, and another is, "Eat not the bread of him who has a hard, grudging and envious eye, neither desire his dainty foods" (Amplified Bible).

When you consider the most prominent translations together, they seem to come out saying something like this: Do not get involved with those who are *unwilling*. Few things in life are as offensive and demoralizing as pouring your life into someone who then balks at paying the lunch check. The proverb writer is telling us not to get enmeshed with those who do not *want* to pull their own weight, economic or otherwise. Some people are determined always to make profit, to come out on top even with their friends. They part with their own resources only grudgingly, as if they were thereby losing a contest if not undergoing death. Involvements with such people can waste a great deal of your time and energy, since you will sometimes spend five hundred dollars of your resources to convince them to part with five dollars of theirs.

Love yourself enough to stay away from the dishonest, to avoid the use of incompetent or otherwise unworthy agents, and to steer clear of those whose hearts are unwilling.

While your work may force you to interact with dishonest people, can you spot them before you get entangled?

Do you choose your agents wisely, aware of how crucial such choices can be?

Do you avoid business involvements with the "unwilling," or in the words of the various translations, of the "evil," the "miserly," the "hard," the "grudging," and the "envious"?

SELF-EVALUATION RATING: 1   2   3   4   5

NOTES AND REFLECTIONS:

GUIDELINE 43

Sometimes mere words are not enough—discipline is needed. For the words may not be heeded (Proverbs 29:19, TLB); In vain is a net spread wide if any bird that flies can see it (Proverbs 1:17, NEB).

Both of these proverbs have to do with the intelligent use of power.

How many times have you been in a store and overheard a parent say something like, "Billy! I told you not to touch that." Billy touches it again. Again the parent says, "Now, Billy. I told you not to touch things on the shelves." Of course, Billy continues to touch whatever he wants.

If the people under you have reason to believe that your words are empty, that you do not intend to back them up with consequences, they will probably ignore anything you say that they do not like. Sometimes they will become "passive aggressive": "Oh, I forgot," or "Sure, I'll get to it, but I've been terribly busy." Other times, they may become overtly rebellious: "Look, I don't see why I have to do that," or even "Get somebody else to do it, because I will not!" I have seen senior executives neutralized by someone who simply said "No." These executives just could not bring themselves to "take names and kick . . ."

Unfortunately, we are all given to occasional laziness and selfishness. One function of a manager is to limit the effects of such moral failings. This does not always have to be done with force and, indeed, punishment should be a last resort. However, unless you are so naturally influential that others eagerly comply with your every wish and whim, you will probably be seen as weak and unworthy of obedience if it looks like you are unwilling to use force when necessary. Others will simply think of you as afraid.

Although we do not like to admit it, much of what we do is governed by observable consequences. How long would you continue to work if you were not paid? How nice would you continue to be with your friends if they started abusing you? How much respect would you really show that superior you do not like, if you could get away with saying everything you felt? Rightly or wrongly, the distribution and redistribution of resources drives much of society along. Your ability to manage people effectively is largely contingent on your ability wisely to grant or to withhold resources.

The second proverb is advising us not to make threats or announce our plans for invoking the powers at our disposal. Sometimes it *is* wise to telegraph such plans, in order to put others on notice. Often, however, it is wiser simply to act when the time is right, without prior warning.

A friend of mine was once appointed to an important job. When he moved into the offices supporting his new position, he inherited a career staff who had seen appointees come and go. When my friend asked the senior staffer to do a few things, he got no results. He asked again, again without effect. Wisely, he waited. A while later, he had to complete a performance evaluation on this staff person, who had continued to ignore his orders and requests. The man came flying in.

"You can't do this. You'll ruin my career." My friend opened his desk drawer and produced a list of everything he had asked the staff person to do. The latter instantly achieved enlightenment, they were able to work out an evaluation both could live with, and my friend never again worried about whether his instructions would be carried out. It is sometimes wise quietly to build your case.

Avoid the potential self-ruin that comes from failing to take necessary corrective action when it is required. Do not make empty threats. Indeed, consider not making threats at all. Just be sure that others *know* that you mean what you say.

Do you sometimes talk when you should act?
Do you sometimes telegraph your moves before making them, when you
    should move unannounced?

SELF-EVALUATION RATING: 1   2   3   4   5

NOTES AND REFLECTIONS:

The wicked are caught in their own violence (Proverbs 21:7, NEB); An evil man is brought down by his wickedness (Proverbs 14:32, NEB); Never rob a helpless man because he is helpless, nor ill-treat a poor wretch in court; for the LORD will take up their cause and rob him who robs them of their livelihood (Proverbs 22:22–23, NEB).

Throughout most of this book we have concentrated on what we might call the human consequences of various actions. I have said very little until now about God.

Is there something that corresponds to what we call providence? Does God actually do things, for example, care for the needy? Is it even true that he "watches over drunks and fools"?

To raise these questions is also to raise what has traditionally been called the problem of evil. When civil disasters claim thousands of lives, including the lives of young children, and indeed when thousands of children and adults die every day of hunger, how can one maintain that there is any benevolent providence to life?

Theologians have debated this question for a long time, and a best-selling book was written by a rabbi who, still believing in God, wanted to understand how God could have allowed the rabbi's son to die from a tragic disease. There are no easy answers to such questions.

It does seem, however, that each of us has to "come down somewhere." Either there is a God or there is not. Either he is benevolent, an idea that is inherent in the very word "God" as we use it, or he is some mixture of good and bad, or perhaps even totally malevolent, with human life his greatest practical joke. While agnosticism is an interesting position to take in the drawing room while we are comfortably sitting by a warm fire, it is not one we can easily carry into the streets, at least not for long. Sooner or later something terrible happens to us or to someone we care about, and then we find ourselves *deciding*.

The proverbs we are now considering are among the most important in this book. Throughout Judeo-Christian history, there has always been a strong conviction that God is loving and that the universe is just. The proverb writers believed that there were cosmic moral laws which one could break only at great expense, and that God would even the score on behalf of those who were victimized. Evil tends to *ensnare* those who do it. Evil is a boomerang! Throw it at someone and it will come back and strike you down.

"Bad guys" who "live by the sword" tend also to "die by the sword." Unscrupulous persons who deal in evil tend, sooner or later, to "fall." People who victimize the defenseless, whether through robbery or legal harassment, will eventually be robbed and perhaps harassed.

Many stories have been written about people who did something terrible, only to end up on the shoals of personal tragedy because of it. Is this mere superstition? Does God care? If he does care, can he, and does he, do anything in our lives? Are we merely waiting for eternity, in hopes that our "scores" will be "adjusted" according to how good or bad we were? Are we only waiting to discover, at the end of the game, that the rules were fair?

The newspapers and entertainment media are even more full of "bad guys finish first" stories. Other than hearing about the occasional murder of some underworld figure, most of us simply do not have any way to observe the MISERY that evil brings to those who do it. Most of this misery is the slow, insidious kind, hardly worthy of the headlines.

Although I do not know *how* God acts, how much through natural laws (including psychosocial ones) and how much through direct intervention, I firmly believe that he *does* work. Dedicate your life to him, be a good guy, and see if he does not help YOU. Will there be "rain" in your life? Probably. "The rain falls on the just and the unjust alike."

Do you avoid violence and predation?
Do you strive for good, or have you become so cynical that you refuse even to try anymore?
If you are cynical, are you willing to ask God to help you soften?

SELF-EVALUATION RATING: 1   2   3   4   5

NOTES AND REFLECTIONS:

PROPER PRIORITIES

GUIDELINE 45

Whoever relies on his wealth is riding for a fall (Proverbs 11:28, NEB); Do not slave to get wealth (Proverbs 23:4, NEB).

Wealth is a tool. Money can provide us with purchasing power, the ability to obtain material things we want as well as services that we need or enjoy, from getting someone to fix the shower to having someone build us a yacht. To become obsessed with money, however, is to confuse the means with the ends. It is to lose sight of the *instrumental* nature of money, that is, to let it become an end. Wealth can NEVER properly be one's ultimate goal. Even if there were no God and no cosmic order, to "slave after money" is to throw away your life in the pursuit of something that is best used to enhance the quality of the life one so foolishly throws away! Since there is a God, to slave after money is to engage in idolatry. We tend to become servants, even *slaves,* of our idols.

God has given each of us a life, a "project of existence" to construct. Our experiences shape us, but we also shape our experiences. We make choices. We make interpretations of events. We have the power to determine, to a large extent, what we become. Success means creating an artful and godly existence. To take the mere accumulation of wealth as proof of success is to mistake a cartoon for a Da Vinci.

These proverbs are telling us not to trust in wealth and not to wear ourselves out (NIV) striving for it. For what, then, should we strive?

We are, by nature, relational beings. We were created to "walk closely" with God and with other people. Good relationships are what bring contentment and peace. Even if we lived alone on an island, we would carry on relationships inside of our minds. We might even carry on audible conversations, perhaps suddenly to remember that we were physically alone. Surely we would carry on mental conversations. Wealth, properly used, is employed to enhance our relationships and our enjoyment of God's creation.

The most important "parts" of creation are people. The worlds of animals, plants, and so on, are indeed beautiful, but their places are trivial in comparison with the world of human beings. The problem is not that we love creation per se too much but that we love it too much in relation to how much we love people. It is the same with money. When you love wealth more than God and people, you run against the currents of every major religion there ever was, including Christianity.

There are some very noble reasons for desiring money, as we noted earlier. One good reason is that a reasonable accumulation of assets makes it unlikely that one will have to worry about whether one can shelter, feed, and clothe oneself and one's loved ones. Money can provide us with a certain kind of security. However, this kind of security is rather limited.

It is freedom from inconvenience and petty hassle, but it is NOT necessarily freedom from loneliness or personal anguish.

The problem with compulsively pursuing money, aside from the adverse physical effects of working too hard, is that such pursuit *distracts* us from the truly important. Some compulsions (e.g., narcotics) and some distractions (e.g., looking at the scenery when we are driving) can prove lethal. Avarice is both a compulsion and a distraction that can be lethal to our psychological and spiritual health.

Do what you can to acquire wealth, but do not let the slave become the master and the master the slave. Every moment of your life is, essentially, a nonrenewable resource. Do not mortgage a present that comes only once for a future that may never come—a future that, even if it does come, is by nature incapable of replacing even one moment that has gone before it.

Money is a tool best used by those who know its limitations as well as its power.

How much do you live each day in the belief that if you only had more money, you would finally be secure?

Are you slaving so hard for wealth that the only thing you are likely to achieve is a massive coronary?

For what exactly do you want more money?

SELF-EVALUATION RATING: 1   2   3   4   5

NOTES AND REFLECTIONS:

Commit to the LORD whatever you do, and your plans will succeed (Proverbs 16:3, NIV).

Have you ever had times in your life when you strongly felt that you were in tune with God and that you were serving him in whatever you were doing? When I have felt like this, life has gone incredibly well. Perhaps we are talking only about emotional experiences. After all, it would not be at all strange for people to get religious when things were going well. Both foxholes and award ceremonies seem to ameliorate atheism. And yet I usually got religious first. The success seemed to follow from that.

The proverb we are considering can quickly be made absurd. Does it mean, for example, that I can get a Ph.D. in nuclear physics if I simply "commit" my plans to God? Surely not. What it does mean, however, is that *great strength* comes from living in union with him. If God is who we think he is, the creator and sustainer of the universe, such living gives us direct access to the real "boss."

If you are reasonably sure that you are doing whatever you are doing out of *commitment* to the Lord, you feel a tremendous sense of power and "centeredness." As a clinical psychologist, I am naturally aware that there are lots of people in the world who claim that God tells them to do everything. But I am not discussing here religiously delusional people but normal people, like you and me, who upon occasion seem to connect with God in a way that straightens things out nicely for us.

Imagine the kind of life we might have if we did everything out of love for him. Imagine the sense of effectiveness you might enjoy if you did all things with a holy commitment. Everything, or nearly everything, would probably fall into place.

Because we are all imperfect, we will never serve God in quite the way I have described. There will always be those times when we forget him or stubbornly choose to go our own way. However, we can at least enact our principal plans with God at their center. We can serve for him, succeed for him.

History provides us with many stories of people whose achievements, by their own description, were done for God. Scientific discoveries, even acts of military heroism (e.g., Sergeant York in World War I), have been done almost as acts of worship. Indeed, I have been amazed at how often the people who seemed most committed to God were also the most committed to excellence. Clearly, there are lots of atheists who have done wonderful things from which society has greatly benefited. Still, people who love God seem more often, to me at least, to "try harder."

If you have lost sight of your alignment with God's purposes, and of how God loves YOU, perhaps because you have been through so many battles and received so many scars, ask him to mellow you out. God may love the downtrodden, but he wants to make all of us into winners. There *can* be winners without losers. Sometimes the choice we have is whether to cling rigidly to our own designs or to surrender our capacity to create designs into his service. Who knows? Maybe God needs someone faithful on the board of General Motors.

How much do your plans reflect a living worship of and faith in God?
When you establish goals, do you pray about them?
Do you actually ask God for his blessings?

SELF-EVALUATION RATING: 1   2   3   4   5

NOTES AND REFLECTIONS:

STAYING OUT IN FRONT

To learn, you must want to be taught (Proverbs 12:1a, TLB); Conceal your faults, and you will not prosper; confess and give them up, and you will find mercy (Proverbs 28:13, NEB).

A few years ago, another psychologist came into my office. "You know," he said, "I really respect you. You're not afraid to put yourself on the line, to put yourself right out there and then take whatever comes, good or bad. You send papers off to the best journals, organize symposia at national conventions, etc. I wish I were more like that." He looked sad, a little forlorn. I was grateful for the compliment but also felt embarrassed. How do you respond to something like this?

The really sad thing is that this psychologist is very gifted. On measures of sheer brainpower, I am quite sure that he would run circles around me. Only he is hesitant to take the risk of criticism. He does not want to bear the pain of someone telling him that he is not perfect. I can identify with this. I used to be like that too. It actually took me a long time and a lot of injured feelings to learn that it is almost always profitable to "put yourself on the line." If you do this often enough, eventually it no longer bothers you—well, most of the time—if someone shoots you a little criticism. So what? Who cares?

Truth is our friend, a hard lesson to remember when we can sense that someone is going to rip us to shreds, perhaps with some justification. We are really dealing here with taking the RISK of discovering truths about ourselves that, initially at least, we would just as soon NOT KNOW. Even if we intellectually understand the value of personal risk-taking, when we are in danger of getting hurt we usually want to put off taking the risk. "I'll find out about myself later, maybe tomorrow. Right now, I don't want to deal with it." To learn, you must want to learn. Sometimes wanting to learn feels like wanting to suffer!

Psychologically, it is extremely difficult to change something about yourself that you have not admitted. Until we come to terms with *exactly* what it is within us that is causing trouble, it is almost impossible to get rid of our self-sabotage systems. This is because most of the self-destructive things we do, we do automatically, without much awareness. In other words, we do them more or less unconsciously. What the writer of the second proverb refers to as confession is closely related to the psychoanalyst's free association, that is, to saying *everything* and not holding back. Obviously you cannot go around all day confessing, but you can talk openly about yourself to a few trusted advisers.

Part of conventional business wisdom is that people who are effective know how to stonewall it and to finesse things. Like the Marines, they never retreat but only "advance in the opposite direction." If you are stonewalling, finessing, or advancing in a new direction for someone else's benefit, you are potentially caught in the tension between truthfulness and loyalty. As far as stonewalling it for yourself, there is certainly a practical advantage to doing so when you are swimming in a pool of hungry sharks. Such is NOT the time to bleed (translation: broadcast one's mistakes). However, there are times to admit one's errors and, in the words of another translation, find "mercy" (TLB: "get another chance").

To refuse ever to discuss your own frailties with anyone is to guarantee that you will never learn very much about yourself. Not to benefit from such insight can be a major weakness, since ultimately what you are selling in business is *you*.

As much as you can, love correction. Using good judgment about where, when, and to whom to reveal yourself, "confess your faults" and, having done that, "give them up."

How much do you believe that truth is your friend?
Do you love correction even when it gives you pain?
Are there people to whom you regularly confess?

SELF-EVALUATION RATING: 1   2   3   4   5

NOTES AND REFLECTIONS:

GUIDELINE 48

Walk with the wise and be wise; mix with the stupid and be misled (Proverbs 13:20, NEB); Never make friends with an angry man nor keep company with a bad-tempered one; be careful not to learn his ways, or you will find yourself caught in a trap (Proverbs 22:24–25, NEB).

Human beings learn a great deal through imitation. We are incredibly adept at picking up the gestures, mannerisms, inflections, and so on, of those around us. The interesting thing is that such learning goes on automatically, without our having to think about it. People from Brooklyn talk a certain way, as do people from Texas. Children whose parents are in the Boston Social Register talk and act differently from those whose parents are factory workers. People from the South usually have different attitudes from people from the North, and both of these have different attitudes from those in the West. Culture, high or low, is largely transmitted through the unconscious imitation of models.

To a considerable extent, we can control the kind of culture we internalize by carefully choosing our associates. If you want erudition, you probably ought to spend time with those who think and speak intellectually. If you want poise, you might consider spending time around those who move and speak with grace. If you want wisdom, associate with the wise.

These proverbs tell us some straightforward things about how to exercise control over what we become. Associate with the wise and, lo and behold, become wise! Associate with the foolish, however, and you will only be misled. If you associate with people who are volatile or even violent, you will probably become like them and, as a result, find yourself "caught in a trap."

Research has shown that, as a rule, even teachers teach as they have been taught, not according to what all their education courses specify. Therapists tend, on the whole, to do with their clients what *their* therapists have done with them, not what they were taught in school or through books. Naturally, nearly everything we do is colored by a number of influences, including formal education, books, and so on. The point remains, however, that perhaps the bulk of what we learn, especially our attitudes, comes through reflexive imitation. Whom we choose to associate with, and thus whom we destine (doom?) ourselves to imitate, is all the more important because attitudes, both stark and subtle, have a tremendous effect on how well we do in the work world.

Now the trick with this guideline is for me somehow to convince you that none of us is immune from the powerful influences of models. I wonder if you do not find yourself saying: "Well, other people may copy what they see and hear, but not me. I think for myself."

I guess all I can do is appeal to my expertise as a psychologist and ask you to believe me when I tell you that *all* of us are far more influenced by models than we care to admit. I do not know to what extent we are "part of all that we have met," but I do know that most of what we have met is part of us. You can only resist so much social influence. Beyond this—and there is much beyond our consciousness—we absorb our environments like sponges.

Select your companions well. Do not let just anybody become your associate. Spend time with others who have ways you want to learn. Do not select people as friends simply because they are like you (which we all tend to do). Choose those who can give you something worthwhile and to whom you can give something of benefit. Those with whom you spend your life become your teachers.

Do the people with whom you spend time demonstrate those qualities you want to develop?

Are there people in your life with whom you should spend less time? More time?

SELF-EVALUATION RATING: 1   2   3   4   5

NOTES AND REFLECTIONS:

GUIDELINE 49

Counsel in another's heart is like deep water, but a discerning man will draw it up (Proverbs 20:5, NEB).

Most people are smart enough to know that when we ask them for their opinions, we usually want to hear praise and confirmation. They automatically, and correctly, translate, "Tell what you really think" into "Tell me what I want, and perhaps desperately need, to hear." We have all learned the hard way, through social punishments like neglect and disapproval, that to take such questions as "How am I doing?" at face value is to invite trouble. So we make our translations and respond accordingly.

If you genuinely WANT to know what others think, you have to get behind their translation devices. Doing this ordinarily means convincing them that you are willing to endure pain, if necessary, to learn the truth. How does one do this?

First, do not ask people to tell you how you are doing when you are down and need support. They will probably sense this need and intelligently provide you with support instead of with truth. If, on the other hand, they actually miss the cues and tell you something unpleasant, you will feel terrible. Ask for truth only when you are in good enough psychological shape to hear it. When you need support, ask for that! Do not hunt tigers when you have only the strength to catch lambs.

Second, ask others specific questions. Think through what you want to know, and frame your questions beforehand. You might try writing them down. You might also ask people to rate you on "1 to 10" with respect to various aspects of performance, such as sensitivity, assertiveness, knowledge, and so on. Some people might even be willing to put some of this in writing for you. The nice thing about having a written document is that you can mull over it at your leisure, when your anxiety is low and you are not sitting face-to-face with the other person. Even if he or she does not want to write anything, you can always take a few notes, even on the back of a napkin. "That's helpful. Let me jot it down."

Third, you might offer to exchange ratings and evaluations. This works best with people who are your equals. You might say something like: "John, I'd like to try something. Let me describe it so you can see if you're willing. Here are some questions. Maybe you could answer them about me and I could do the same for you. Or, if you prefer, you can just answer them for me." Many people would be willing at least to do the latter.

Let me suggest some possible questions:

1. What do you see as my major strengths?
2. What do you see as my major weaknesses?
3. How much of a problem do these weaknesses represent?

4. Are there specific things I should be doing?
5. Are there things I am doing that I shouldn't be?
6. If I continue on my present course, where do you see me in five years, ten years, twenty years?

You can probably come up with questions that are better for you, ones that more specifically address whatever concerns about yourself you may have. I hope these questions will at least serve to get you started. Go easy at first. If you have not done this sort of thing before, you will probably find it very frightening when you actually get down to doing it. Start with the easy questions!

Is there someone with whom you might exchange constructive evaluations?
What questions would you most like answered?

SELF-EVALUATION RATING: 1   2   3   4   5

NOTES AND REFLECTIONS:

GUIDELINE 50

To learn sense is true self-love; cherish discernment and make sure of success (Proverbs 19:8, NEB).

To love yourself in the best and highest sense probably requires that you come to grips with God's love for you. YOU are his beloved creature, the apex of his creation. God has invested in you by giving you a life.

Please do not confuse what I am saying with some of the self-love talk floating around. Some of the most obnoxious people I have met are members of the navel-gazing cult, devotees of the "me first" mythology. The object of life is NOT simply to love yourself but to love God and serve people. Life is a training academy for holiness. The whole point of the game is that we become ever more like God, in other words, that we become more loving and more just. Our very minds are designed to expand in such a way that we can, as it were, think like God. But how does God think?

God has sense! This may sound silly, so let me explain. He is very good at telling the difference between right and wrong, for example, and between real love and feigned love. And so on. We need to come to see with his eyes. To do this is, for us, to acquire sense. The proverb writer tells us that by acquiring sense we will make sure of our own success.

What, however, *is* success? We have already noted that success is far more than money, which at best is a tool and in our baser moments the way we "keep score." Let me close our last guideline discussion with a statement about what I believe success includes:

> To succeed is to grow ever closer to God and other people; to discover and exercise the gifts God has given us and, thus, to do the best we can with what we have; to face life with courage, committed to learning such truths about God and ourselves as we can, refusing to hide; to live with a pure heart, wanting our own and others' good; to be contented with what we have, trying always to make life better for everyone.

It is perhaps not very helpful to say that success is being everything that God intends us to be, since that leaves us with the question of determining exactly what he intends. Still, I find it personally helpful to ask, "What does he want *me* to be?" Being able to answer this question is perhaps the essence of "sense." Bear in mind, however, that some of what we may think God wants may be nothing more than false expectations that have been drummed into us by others.

"Happy is he who has found wisdom, and the man who has acquired understanding; for wisdom is more profitable than silver, and the gain she brings is better than gold" (3:13–14, NEB). The search for God and his holiness is the beginning of the path to wisdom.

It is so much harder to quest after something intangible, like sense, than something we can see and touch, like a new house or a better television. Yet all the really important things in life—love, joy, peace, and so on—are by nature intangible. To seek only what we can see with our senses is to show very little sense.

Go for it! "It" can stand for just about anything, from becoming president to making a few billion. There is nothing wrong, and a good deal right, with success as it is conventionally defined. Just be careful that *your* definition of success is more enlightened and expanded than the traditional one, which translates it only into dollar signs and status symbols. Seek the bigger success of following God and "all these things will be added unto you."

How do you define success for yourself?
When you get to the end of your life and look back, what do you want to
  be able to say?

SELF-EVALUATION RATING: 1   2   3   4   5

NOTES AND REFLECTIONS:

CONCLUSION

Let us review some of the teachings contained in our fifty guidelines. While obviously we cannot summarize everything in a few paragraphs, I would like to put into condensed form some of the more important teachings that we have considered:

Your words have powerful effects. Use them to win friends, especially to make others look as good as they can. Avoid conflict whenever possible. Listen carefully to questions before giving answers. Quietly give well-chosen gifts. Pay your debts, and be fair. Do not hide your love or appreciation; express it. Use your intelligence for good, so that others will like you. Develop patience; don't be impulsive. On the other hand, don't be afraid to take intelligent business risks either. Recognize others' power. Be careful in choosing whom you try to rescue, or for whom you will countersign. Whenever you can, suspend judgment until you have enough proof. Hard work still works! Attention to detail is sometimes the road to advancement. Plan thoroughly. Learn to save and invest as a way of life. Keep your speech appropriate; avoid chronic complaining. Don't talk too much. Do not always say everything but select what is best to say. Share your wisdom only with people who want to hear it. Silence can even make you look wise. Be modest, not pretentious. Keep open-minded. Pay attention to what others try to tell you. Watch out for pride and arrogance. People have different gifts: discover and use yours. Speak truthfully. Confrontation sometimes pays off in the long run. An honest heart breeds contentment. Be wary of fading charms and beauties; honor your own loved one. Build up an estate for your dependents. Overlook minor faults. Consider the consequences before you pledge or sign. Watch out for trouble and avoid it. Develop your business before your indulgences. Avoid practical jokes or the use of humor to excuse hostility. Honor the confidences of others. Do not wear out your welcome. Speak graciously, honestly, and nonmaliciously. Keep away from unsavory associates or unsuitable agents. Back up what you say. God protects the weak, so don't prey on them. Use whatever wealth you have for good, but do not place too much trust in your money or become its slave. Commit your plans to God. Be open, when the time is right, about your mistakes. Actively but prudently seek others' evaluations. Spend time with those whose virtues you would like to acquire, especially those with special wisdom. Live for God.

God wants us to do well and he has given us the book of Proverbs for our guidance. I am confident that your "performance" will improve if you attend to its teachings, adapting them appropriately to your own circumstances.

RATE YOURSELF

Add up your fifty scores (maximum total=250). Rate yourself on the guidelines again in a month and see if your total score indicates improvement. Use the table below, if convenient, to record your totals.

DATE	POINT TOTAL	GUIDELINES WITH LOW RATINGS

SUGGESTED READING

Since there is always merit to "knowing what you are up against," I recommend that you read *other* self-help books, such as Robert Ringer's *Winning Through Intimidation* (Los Angeles Book Publishing Co., 2d ed., 1974) and Michael Korda's *Power: How to Get It, How to Use It* (Random House, 1975).

If I had to recommend one book that is both very wise and very godly, it would be Robert Greenleaf's *Servant Leadership* (Paulist Press, 1977). Greenleaf was the director of management research for the largest private sector employer in the world, AT&T. His book, by his own description, is about "legitimate power and greatness."